TRANSLATE THE COMMUNIST MANIFESTO,
SPREAD THE IDEA OF MARXISM

宣言中译 信仰之源

《共产党宣言》展示馆（陈望道旧居）

复旦大学档案馆 编

复旦大学出版社

序

　　陈望道先生是我国马克思主义的早期传播者,《共产党宣言》首位中文全译本翻译者,中国共产党创始人之一,同时也是著名学者和教育家,是新中国成立后复旦大学的首任校长。坐落于国福路51号的复旦玖园曾是陈望道先生的旧居。2018年,值马克思诞辰200周年、《共产党宣言》发表170周年之际,我们以"信仰之源"为主题,将陈望道故居打造成《共产党宣言》展示馆,致敬大师、重温经典。如今,展示馆已经成为党史和复旦校史的教育基地,也已成为上海乃至全国的红色地标。

　　追望大道,求索不息。1920年8月,由陈望道翻译的第一个中文全译本《共产党宣言》在上海出版,为中国共产党的应运而生奠定了重要的思想理论基础。毛泽东、周恩来、朱德、邓小平等老一辈革命家都曾言及这一译本的重要价值,习近平总书记也曾多次提起"真理的味道",讲述陈望道先生专注译书、把墨水当红糖吃的故事。1920年9月,陈望道开始在复旦大学任教。同年年底,陈望道接任《新青年》主编,把刊物作为思想舆论阵地,大力传播马克思主义,宣传反帝反封建思想。陈望道参加了早期党的创建工作,建党后,被任命为中国共产党上海地方委员会书记。抗战时期,复旦内迁北碚,陈望道时任新闻系主任,在炮火中竖起"好学力行"大旗,带领师生坚持真理、追求进步,复旦成为大后方的"民主堡垒",被中共南方局誉为"学校工作的典型和模范"。1952年至1977年,陈望道担任复旦大学校长,为社会主义大学建设呕心沥血。他"信仰共产主义终身不变"的铮铮誓言，为复旦学脉注入了赓续百年的红色基因。

信仰恒在，历久弥新。今年是望道老校长翻译出版《共产党宣言》首个中文全译本100周年，我们将《共产党宣言》展示馆的重要图文资料编印成册，以飨读者。画册系统展示了《共产党宣言》中文全译本诞生、刊行、传播的全过程，以及对中国革命和革命者的巨大影响。画册也忠实还原了望道先生一生的精神追求、道德文章及品格风范，希望能让"真理的味道"更广传播，让信仰的力量更加凝聚。

习近平总书记指出，中国共产党是《共产党宣言》精神的忠实传人。在纪念《共产党宣言》中译百年之际，复旦大学倍加珍惜望老留下的宝贵精神财富，将进一步传承弘扬红色基因，做宣言精神的忠实传人，把"真理的味道"的故事一代代讲下去，努力培养更多的社会主义合格建设者和接班人，不辜负党和国家重托，不辜负人民的厚望！

复旦大学党委书记 焦扬

2020年4月

目录

宣言中译 信仰之源	千秋巨笔 一代宗师	玖园一隅 好学力行
红色经典　2	光辉一生　66	大师望道　109
信仰之源　5	静穆书房　72	真理味道　112
不忘初心　46	睹物思人　76	字字珠玑　114
又新出版　49	复旦印记　87	国福路51号　115
版本阅读　51	精神财富　100	结语　118
	书香留芳　104	
	珍藏手迹　106	

宣言中译　信仰之源

TRANSLATING *THE COMMUNIST MANIFESTO*, SPREADING THE IDEAL OF MARXISM

宣言中译　信仰之源

红色经典　MARXISM CLASSICS

● 序厅（原为旧居一楼的复旦大学语言研究室）

「前 言」

- 《共产党宣言》是国际共产主义运动的第一个纲领性文献，第一次完整、系统地阐述了马克思主义的科学社会主义基本理论、基本思想。它的发表标志着马克思主义的诞生，深刻影响了人类历史进程。1920年8月，陈望道所译《共产党宣言》第一个中文全译本问世，为中国共产党的创建作了重要的思想理论准备。

- 陈望道是中国共产党最早的党员之一，曾担任中共上海地方委员会首任书记。1920年到复旦任教，历任中国文学教员、中文系主任、新闻系主任、文学院院长。1952年到1977年任复旦大学校长。他毕生从事文化教育事业，成就卓著。他是学术大师，教育名家。

- 这栋小楼的二、三层曾是陈望道1956年到1977年在复旦大学的寓所。旧居于2014年入选上海市文物保护单位，由中共上海市委宣传部和复旦大学发起，上海市教育委员会和上海市教育发展基金会参与，辟建为《共产党宣言》展示馆，作为复旦大学校史馆专题馆，长设"宣言中译 信仰之源"主题教育展。

前言 Prologue

《共产党宣言》是国际共产主义运动的第一个纲领性文献，第一次完整、系统地阐述了马克思主义的科学社会主义基本理论、基本思想。它的发表标志着马克思主义的诞生，深刻影响了人类历史进程。1920年春，陈望道第一次把《共产党宣言》全文译成中文，为中国共产党的创建作了重要的思想理论准备。

陈望道是中国共产党最早的党员之一，曾担任中共上海地方委员会首任书记。1920年到复旦任教，历任中国文学教员、中文系主任、新闻系主任、文学院院长。1952年到1977年任复旦大学校长。他毕生从事文化教育事业，成就卓著。

这栋小楼的二、三层曾是陈望道1956年到1977年在复旦大学的寓所。旧居于2014年入选上海市文物保护单位。由中共上海市委宣传部和复旦大学发起，上海市教育委员会和上海市教育发展基金会参与，辟建为《共产党宣言》展示馆，作为复旦大学校史馆专题馆，长设"宣言中译 信仰之源"主题教育展。

The *Communist Manifesto* as the first programmatic document for the international communist movement, fully and systematically elaborated the fundamental theories and conceptions of scientific socialism. The publication of the *Manifesto* marked the birth of Marxism, and since then Marxism had been profoundly influencing the development of the whole human history. In the spring of 1920, Mr. Chen Wangdao initially and originally translated the *Manifesto* into modern Chinese version as the ideological pillar for the establishment of the Communist Party of China (CPC).

Mr. Chen Wangdao was one of the founding members of CPC, and served as the first Secretary of Shanghai Provincial Party Committee of the CPC. He began to teach in Fudan University since 1920, and served as Director of the Department of Chinese Language and Literature, Director of the Department of Journalism. From 1952 to 1977, he served as President of Fudan University. He dedicated himself to inheriting and promoting Chinese culture, and also one of the most outstanding scholars and educators in modern China.

This is the house where Mr. Chen Wangdao lived from 1956 to 1977, he lived on the second and third floor. The house was selected as a cultural heritage site protected by Shanghai Municipal Government from 2014. Now it serves to the public as the theme pavilion of Fudan University History Museum to exhibit the *Manifesto* as the stationary special exhibition of *the Source of Belief*.

宣言中译　信仰之源

「PROLOGUE」

- *The Communist Manifesto* is the first programmatic document for the international communist movement, which systematically elaborates the fundamental theories and conceptions of scientific socialism. The publication of *The Manifesto* marks the birth of Marxism, and since then Marxism has profoundly influenced the development of the whole human history. In the August of 1920, the first complete Chinese version of *The Communist Manifesto* translated by Chen Wangdao was published. It has been the important theoretical preparation for the founding of the Communist Party of China (CPC).

- Mr. Chen was one of the founding members of the CPC, and also served as the first Secretary of the Shanghai Chapter of the CPC. He began to teach Chinese literature at Fudan University in 1920, and later was appointed Head of the Department of Chinese Language and Literature, Head of the Department of Journalism, and Dean of the Faculty of Arts successively. From 1952 to 1977, he was President of Fudan University. He dedicated himself to promoting Chinese culture, and was also one of the most outstanding scholars and educators in modern China.

- This is the very building where Mr. Chen lived from 1956 to 1977. The building was selected as a cultural heritage site protected by Shanghai Municipal Government in 2014. Now it is open to the public as the theme exhibition of Fudan University History Museum to exhibit various editions of *The Communist Manifesto*.

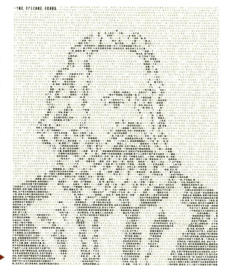 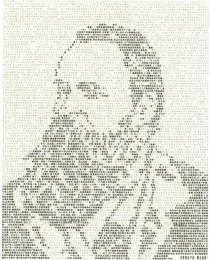

原中央编译局编辑了由《共产党宣言》中文全文组成的马恩头像宣传品 ▶

SOURCE OF BELIEF 信仰之源

宣言中译　信仰之源

● 宣言大厅（原为旧居一楼的复旦大学语言研究室）

— 宣言中译　信仰之源 —

「序」

- 这是一部闪耀着真理光辉的划时代文献。两位不满30岁的青年作者，以睿智的目光，穿透欧洲的黑夜，洞明人类社会发展的客观规律，指引改变世界的伟大革命实践。

- 这部文献就是1848年2月在伦敦发表、由马克思和恩格斯撰写的《共产党宣言》。

- 1920年8月，首个《共产党宣言》中文全译本在上海出版，由时年29岁的陈望道参照日文版和英文版翻译完成。这册只有56页的普通32开中译本，不到两万字，却给苦难中寻求光明的中国人带来了全新的世界观和方法论。译本出版不到一年，中国共产党在上海诞生。

- 《共产党宣言》深刻影响了人类历史的进程，深刻影响了中国的命运。

▲ 1948年俄文纪念版《共产党宣言》中刊登的青年马克思、恩格斯素描像

▲ 1948年俄文纪念版《共产党宣言》

宣言中译　信仰之源

FOREWORD

- This is an epoch-making document glittering with the glory of truth. Two young German philosophers who were less than 30 years old saw through the darkness of the nights in Europe with profound insights, and set forth their positions in foreseeing the future development of the human society. As a result, this document became a beacon of hope to the future revolutions that would change the world fundamentally.

- The document is *The Communist Manifesto*, a political pamphlet penned by Karl Marx and Friedrich Engels, commissioned by the Communist League, and originally published in London in February 1848.

- In August 1920, the first complete Chinese version of *The Manifesto* was published in Shanghai. Mr. Chen Wangdao, who was then 29 years old, translated *The Manifesto* into Chinese completely from both the Japanese and English versions. This first Chinese version brought the totally new world view and methodology to the Chinese people fumbling in the dark. Less than one year after its publication, the Communist Party of China was established in Shanghai.

- *The Manifesto* has profoundly influenced the development of the human history, especially that of China.

▲ 1920年8月首个《共产党宣言》中文全译本诞生

宣言中译　信仰之源

「诞生：阶级使命　人类解放」
BIRTH: THE MISSION OF THE PROLETARIAT, HUMAN EMANCIPATION

- 19世纪上半叶，欧洲资本主义迅速发展，无产阶级与资产阶级的矛盾日趋尖锐。英、法、德等国工人运动风起云涌，无产阶级作为独立的政治力量开始登上了历史舞台。时代呼唤能够指导国际工人运动的科学理论和实践纲领，呼唤用科学理论武装起来的无产阶级革命政党。

- In the early 19th century, European capitalism rapidly developed, and the conflict between the proletariat and the bourgeoisie gradually intensified. Workers' movements in Britain, France, Germany and other countries escalated. As a consequence, the proletariat started to appear on the historical stage as an independent political power. The era called for scientific theories and practical guidelines that could guide the international workers' movement, and it also called a revolutionary proletarian party equipped with scientific theories.

- 《共产党宣言》是马克思和恩格斯受共产主义者同盟委托起草的纲领。1848年2月在英国伦敦出版单行本。《宣言》用历史唯物主义观点阐明了人类社会发展规律和阶级斗争学说，揭示了资本主义的内在矛盾，论证了资本主义的必然灭亡和共产主义的必然胜利，阐述了无产阶级的伟大历史使命，为无产阶级及其政党的革命实践活动提供了强大的精神武器。

- Upon the request of the Communist League of historical materialism, Karl Marx and Friedrich Engels wrote *The Communist Manifesto*, which was published in London in February 1848. From the perspective of historical materialism, *The Communist Manifesto* elaborated the laws of the development of the human society and the theory of class struggles, revealed the internal contradictions of capitalism, and argued for the inevitable fall of the bourgeoisie and the victory of the proletariat. It also expounded on the great historical mission of the proletarians, and provided a powerful spiritual weapon for the proletariat and its political party for their revolutionary practice.

《共产党宣言》的要旨
Key Points of *The Communist Manifesto*

• 《共产党宣言》论述了共产党的性质、特点、基本纲领和策略原则，奠定了马克思主义建党学说的基础，是马克思主义诞生的重要标志。《宣言》批判了当时流行的各种社会主义流派，划清了科学共产主义和这些流派的界限，并提出了"全世界无产者，联合起来！"这一战斗口号。

• *The Communist Manifesto*, marking the birth of Marxism, discusses the nature, the characteristics, the basic program and the strategic principles of the Communist Party. It establishes the foundation upon which Marxist parties should be built. *The Manifesto* criticizes the different socialist schools popular at that time, distinguishes scientific communism from these schools, and puts forward the rallying cry "Working men of all countries, unite!"

• 在陆续被译成法、英、俄等多种语言的过程中，马克思、恩格斯为《共产党宣言》的不同版本写下了七篇序言，对《宣言》做了与时俱进的补充、修正和导读，成为《宣言》的有机组成部分。

• As *The Manifesto* was translated into different languages such as French, English, and Russian, Marx and Engels wrote seven prefaces to its various versions. These prefaces provided necessary supplementation, modification and introduction, thus becoming an integral part of *The Manifesto*.

宣言中译　信仰之源

• 贯穿《共产党宣言》的基本思想：每一历史时代的经济生产以及必然由此产生的社会结构，是该时代政治的和精神的历史基础，因此（从原始土地公有制解体以来）全部历史都是阶级斗争的历史，即社会发展各个阶段上被剥削阶级和剥削阶级之间、被统治阶级和统治阶级之间斗争的历史……这个基本思想完全是属于马克思一个人的。

——弗·恩格斯1883年德文版序言，1883年6月28日于伦敦

• The basic thought running through *The Manifesto* - that economic production, and the structure of society of every historical epoch necessarily arising therefrom, constitute the foundation for the political and intellectual history of that epoch; that consequently (ever since the dissolution of the primeval communal ownership of land) all history has been a history of class struggles, of struggles between exploited and exploiting, between dominated and dominating classes at various stages of social evolution ... this basic thought belongs solely and exclusively to Marx.

— Friedrich Engels wrote in the preface to the 1883 German version, June 28, 1883, London

• 《共产党宣言》的历史在很大程度上反映着现代工人运动的历史；现在，它无疑是全部社会主义文献中传播最广和最带国际性的著作，是从西伯利亚起到加利福尼亚止的千百万工人公认的共同纲领。

虽然《宣言》是我们两人共同的作品，但我认为自己有责任指出，构成《宣言》核心的基本原理是属于马克思的。……这一思想在我看来必定会对历史学做出像达尔文学说对生物学那样的贡献……

——弗·恩格斯1888年英文版序言，1888年1月30日于伦敦

• Thus the history of *The Manifesto* reflects the history of the modern working class movement; at present, it is doubtless the most widespread, the most international production of all socialist literature, the common platform acknowledged by millions of working men from Siberia to California.

The Manifesto being our joint production, I consider myself bound to state that the fundamental proposition which forms the nucleus belongs to Marx ... This proposition, which, in my opinion, is destined to do for history what Darwin's theory has done for biology ...

— Friedrich Engels wrote in the preface to the 1888 English version, January 30, 1888, London

宣言中译　信仰之源

1.《共产党宣言》
丹麦语，1971年版

2.《共产党宣言》
法文，1901年版

3.《共产党宣言》
意大利文，1948年版

4.《共产党宣言》
英文，1915年版

5. 1848年首版《共产党宣言》
德文，1978年纪念版

6.《共产党宣言》
弗拉芒文（荷兰），1917年版

―― 宣言中译　信仰之源 ――

「共震：华夏命运　道路抉择」
PURSUING: THE FUTURE OF CHINA, THE CHOICE OF THE NATION

• 鸦片战争后，中国陷入内忧外患的黑暗境地，中国人民经历了战乱频仍、山河破碎、民不聊生的深重苦难。为了民族复兴，无数仁人志士不屈不挠、前赴后继，进行了可歌可泣的斗争，进行了各式各样的尝试，但终究未能改变旧中国的社会性质和中国人民的悲惨命运。

• After the Opium War, China fell into the despair of domestic revolt and foreign invasion. The Chinese people experienced unspeakable anguish – the terror of wars, the destruction of their homeland, and economic hardships. In order to rebuild their nation, numerous people went through unyielding, continuous, and heroic struggles, but after countless tries, they still failed to transform the nature of old Chinese society and the tragic fate of the Chinese people.

宣言中译　信仰之源

- 十月革命一声炮响，给中国送来了马克思列宁主义。中国先进分子从马克思列宁主义的科学真理中看到了解决中国问题的出路。在近代以后中国社会的剧烈运动中，在中国人民反抗封建统治和外来侵略的激烈斗争中，在马克思列宁主义同中国工人运动的结合过程中，1921年中国共产党应运而生。从此，中国人民谋求民族独立、人民解放和国家富强、人民幸福的斗争就有了主心骨，中国人民就从精神上由被动转为主动。

- After the October Revolution, Marxism-Leninism was introduced into China. Enlightened people in China found a way to solve China's problems through the scientific truth of Marxism-Leninism. The emergence of communism in China in 1921 was a result of intensive movements in modern times, the intense struggle of Chinese people's resistance to the feudalist rule and foreign invasion, and the process of integration between Marxism-Leninism and Chinese workers' movements. Therefrom, hope emerged in the struggle of Chinese people in seeking national independence, people's liberation, national prosperity, and people's happiness, and the spirit of Chinese people changed from passive to proactive.

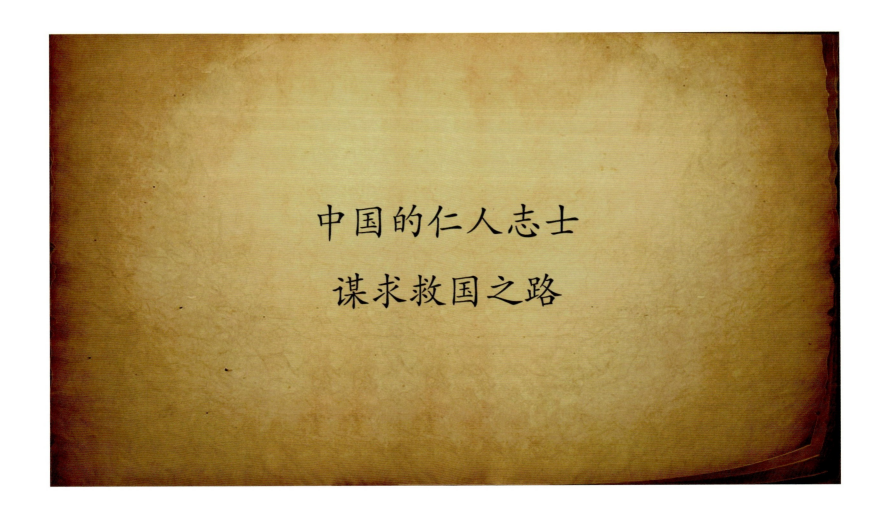

中国的仁人志士
谋求救国之路

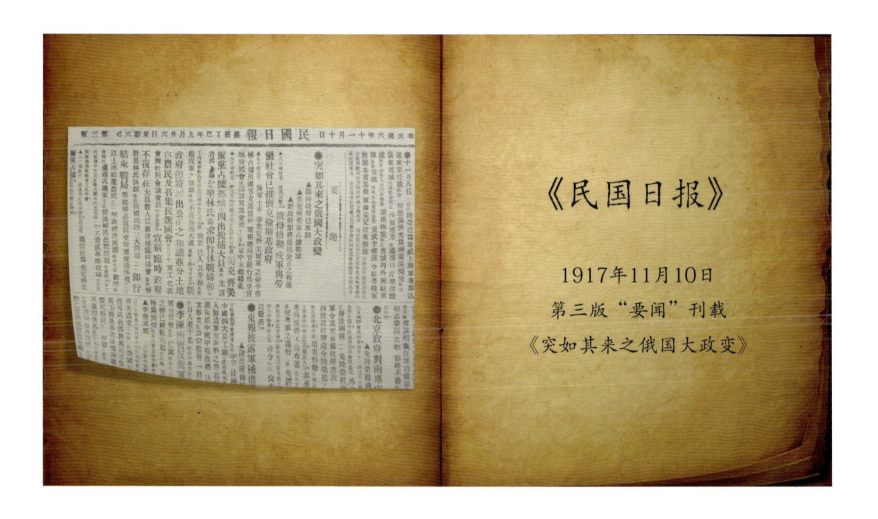

《民国日报》

1917年11月10日

第三版"要闻"刊载

《突如其来之俄国大政变》

宣言中译　信仰之源

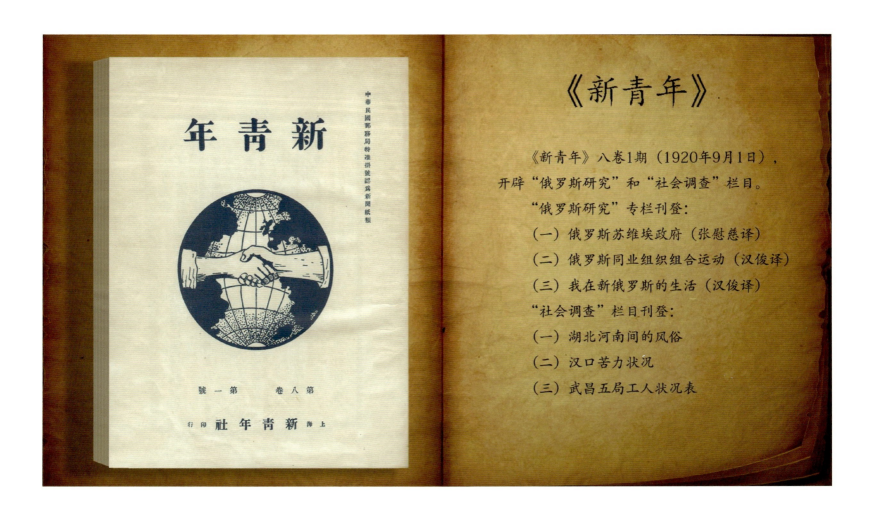

《新青年》

《新青年》八卷1期（1920年9月1日），开辟"俄罗斯研究"和"社会调查"栏目。

"俄罗斯研究"专栏刊登：

（一）俄罗斯苏维埃政府（张慰慈译）

（二）俄罗斯同业组织组合运动（汉俊译）

（三）我在新俄罗斯的生活（汉俊译）

"社会调查"栏目刊登：

（一）湖北河南间的风俗

（二）汉口苦力状况

（三）武昌五局工人状况表

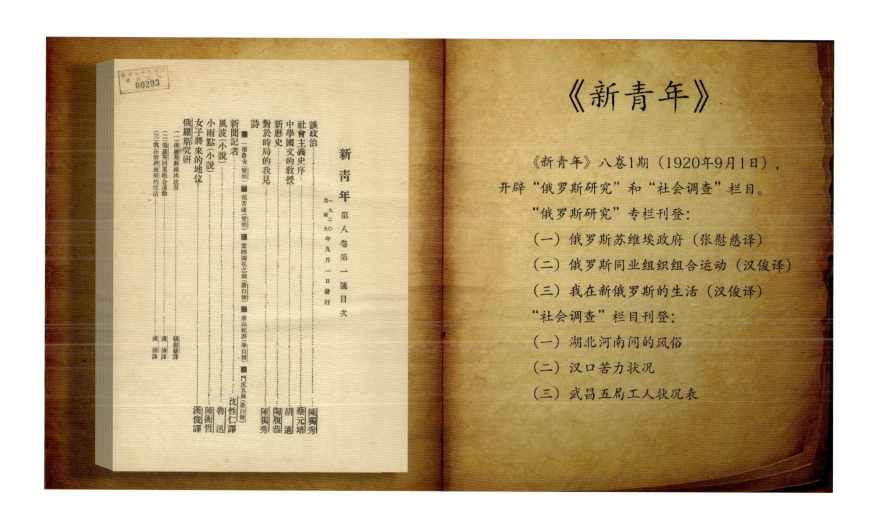

《新青年》

《新青年》八卷1期（1920年9月1日），开辟"俄罗斯研究"和"社会调查"栏目。

"俄罗斯研究"专栏刊登：

（一）俄罗斯苏维埃政府（张慰慈译）

（二）俄罗斯同业组织组合运动（汉俊译）

（三）我在新俄罗斯的生活（汉俊译）

"社会调查"栏目刊登：

（一）湖北河南间的风俗

（二）汉口苦力状况

（三）武昌五局工人状况表

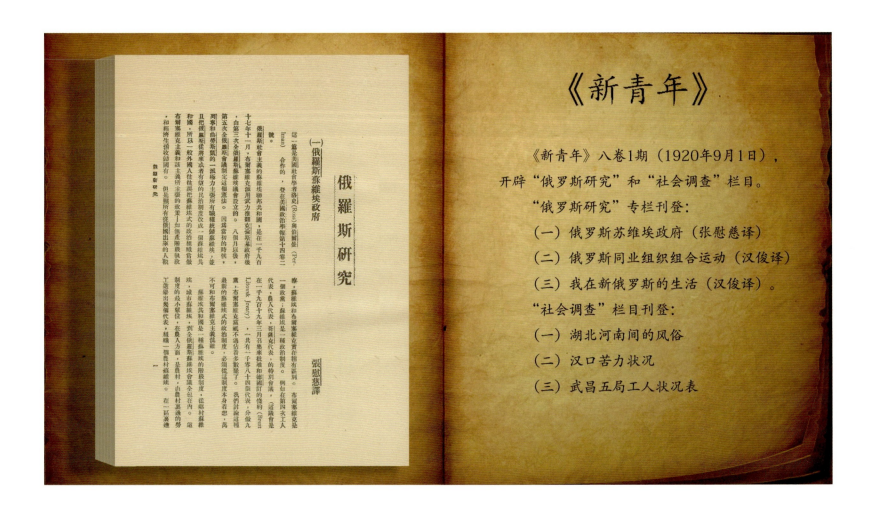

《新青年》

《新青年》八卷1期（1920年9月1日），开辟"俄罗斯研究"和"社会调查"栏目。

"俄罗斯研究"专栏刊登：

（一）俄罗斯苏维埃政府（张慰慈译）

（二）俄罗斯同业组织组合运动（汉俊译）

（三）我在新俄罗斯的生活（汉俊译）。

"社会调查"栏目刊登：

（一）湖北河南间的风俗

（二）汉口苦力状况

（三）武昌五局工人状况表

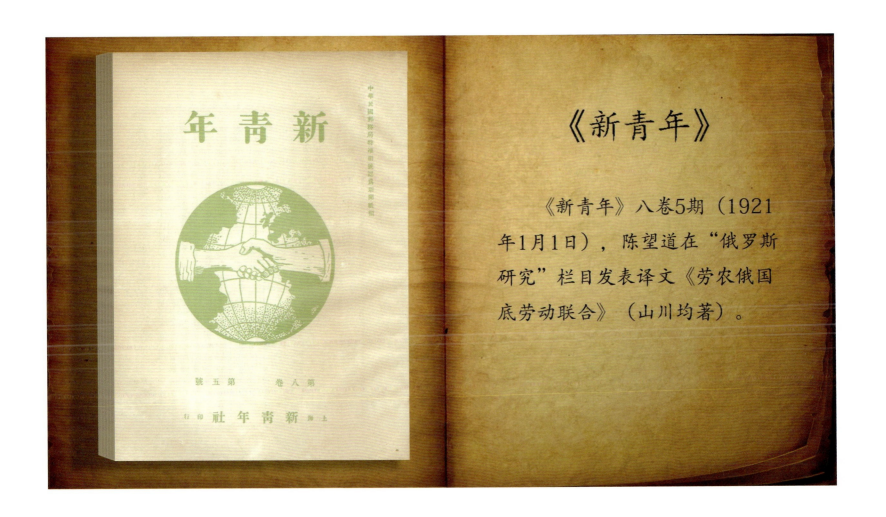

《新青年》

《新青年》八卷5期（1921年1月1日），陈望道在"俄罗斯研究"栏目发表译文《劳农俄国底劳动联合》（山川均著）。

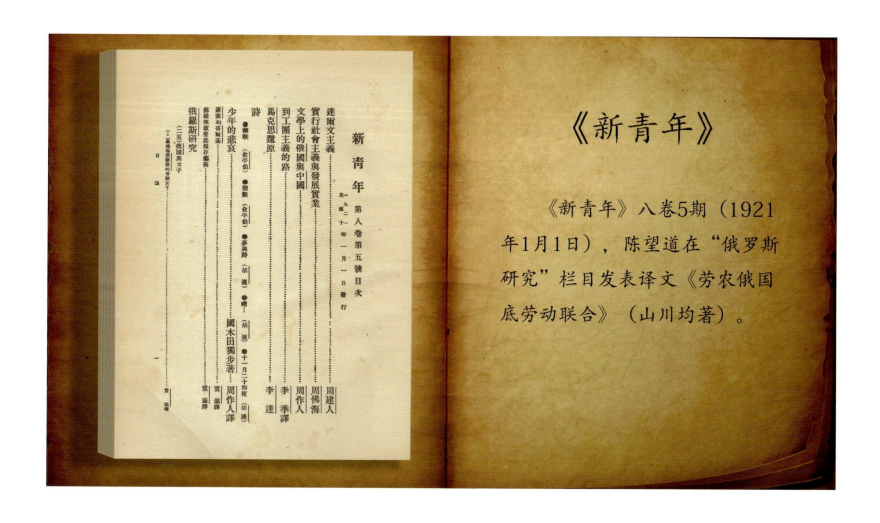

《新青年》

《新青年》八卷5期（1921年1月1日），陈望道在"俄罗斯研究"栏目发表译文《劳农俄国底劳动联合》（山川均著）。

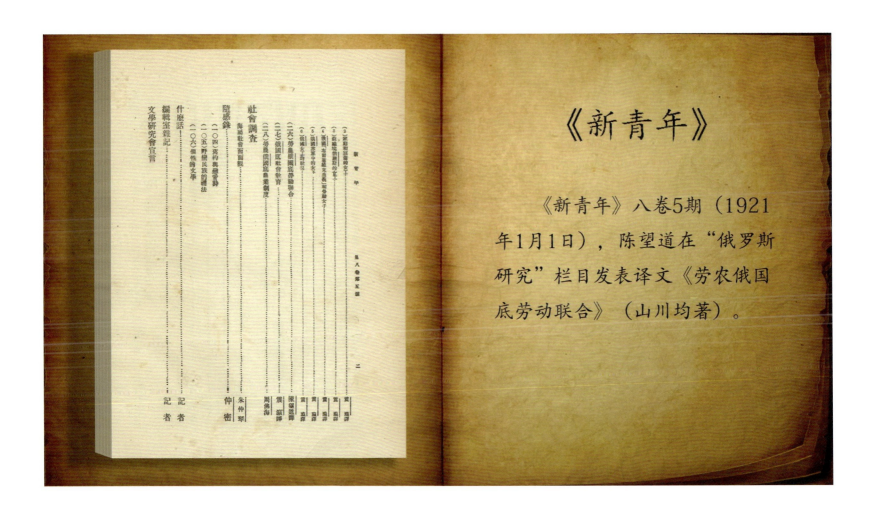

《新青年》

《新青年》八卷5期（1921年1月1日），陈望道在"俄罗斯研究"栏目发表译文《劳农俄国底劳动联合》（山川均著）。

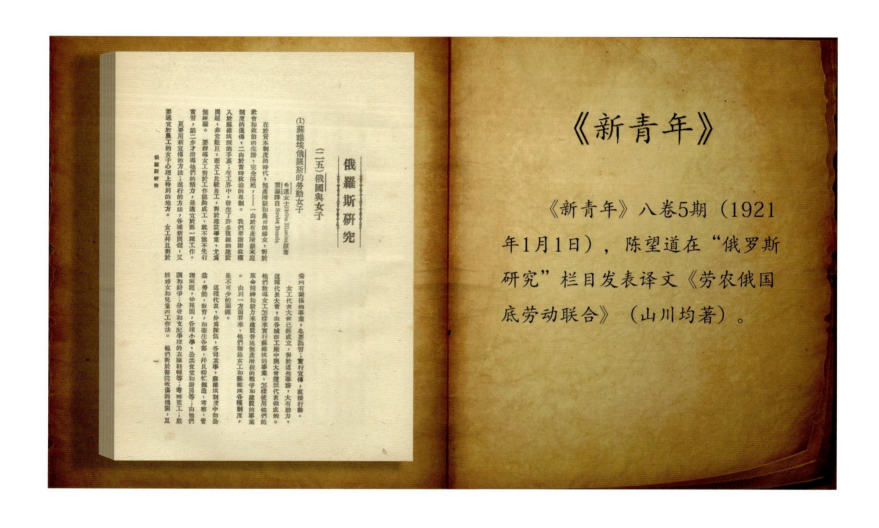

《新青年》

《新青年》八卷5期（1921年1月1日），陈望道在"俄罗斯研究"栏目发表译文《劳农俄国底劳动联合》（山川均著）。

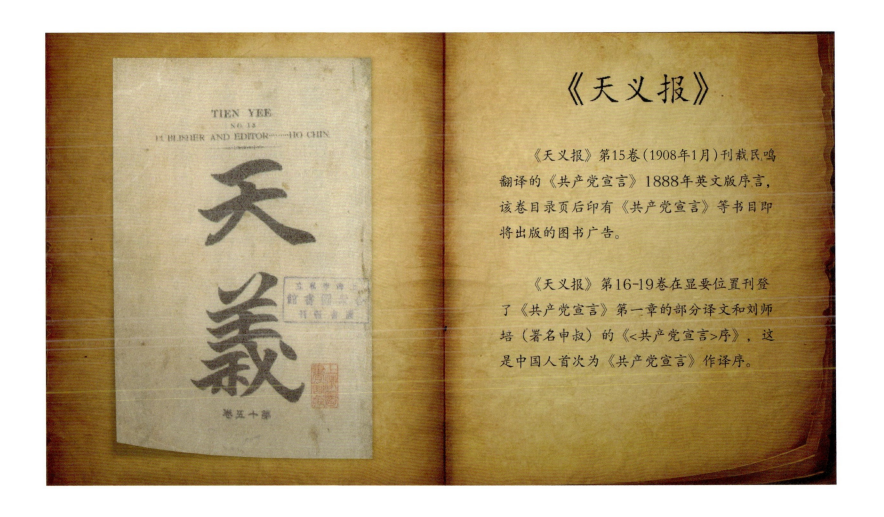

《天义报》

《天义报》第15卷（1908年1月）刊载民鸣翻译的《共产党宣言》1888年英文版序言，该卷目录页后印有《共产党宣言》等书目即将出版的图书广告。

《天义报》第16-19卷在显要位置刊登了《共产党宣言》第一章的部分译文和刘师培（著名申叔）的《<共产党宣言>序》，这是中国人首次为《共产党宣言》作译序。

宣言中译　信仰之源

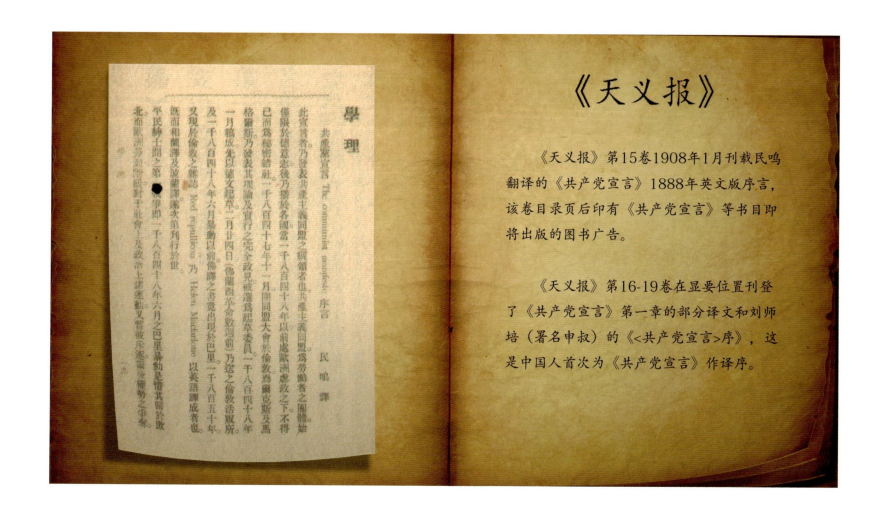

《天义报》

《天义报》第15卷1908年1月刊载民鸣翻译的《共产党宣言》1888年英文版序言，该卷目录页后印有《共产党宣言》等书目即将出版的图书广告。

《天义报》第16-19卷在显要位置刊登了《共产党宣言》第一章的部分译文和刘师培（署名申叔）的《<共产党宣言>序》，这是中国人首次为《共产党宣言》作译序。

《天义报》

《天义报》第15卷（1908年1月）刊载民鸣翻译的《共产党宣言》1888年英文版序言，该卷目录页后印有《共产党宣言》等书目即将出版的图书广告。

《天义报》第16—19卷在显要位置刊登了《共产党宣言》第一章的部分译文和刘师培（署名申叔）的《〈共产党宣言〉序》，这是中国人首次为《共产党宣言》作译序。

宣言中译　信仰之源

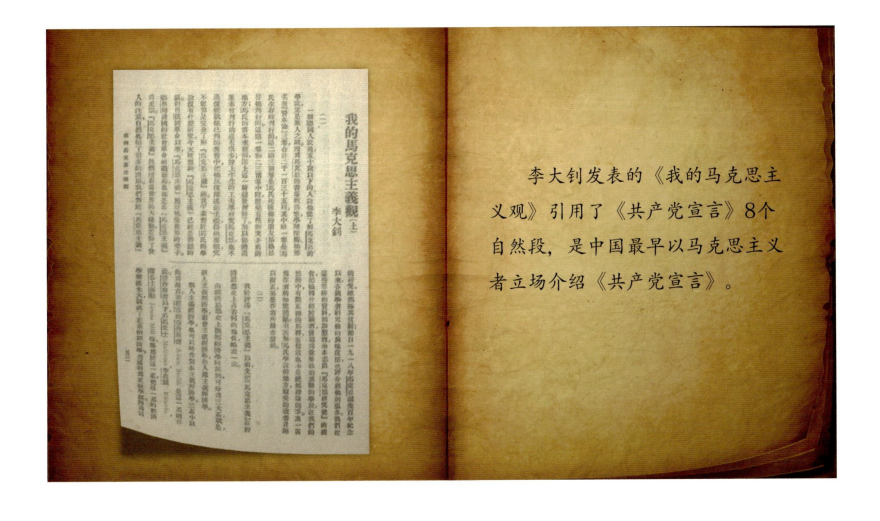

李大钊发表的《我的马克思主义观》引用了《共产党宣言》8个自然段,是中国最早以马克思主义者立场介绍《共产党宣言》。

《每周评论》

《每周评论》
第16号（1919年4月）
发表成舍我著的《共产党的宣言》

宣言中译　信仰之源

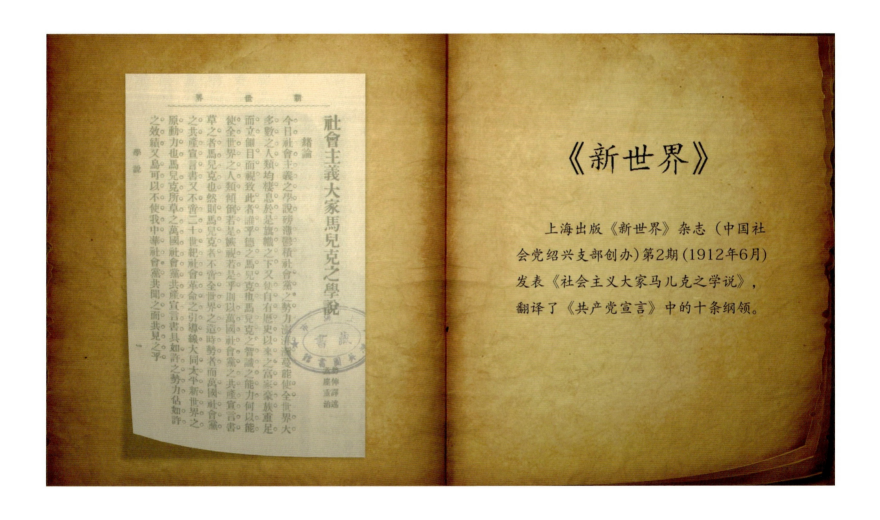

《新世界》

上海出版《新世界》杂志（中国社会党绍兴支部创办）第2期（1912年6月）发表《社会主义大家马儿克之学说》，翻译了《共产党宣言》中的十条纲领。

宣言中译　信仰之源

▲ 陈望道学籍展柜

▲ 陈望道在日本求学期间接触到的马克思主义读物

▲ 1916年9月至1917年5月陈望道（注册姓名陈融）就读于日本早稻田大学法科

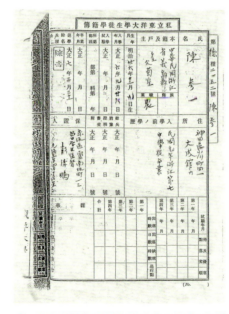
▲ 1917年9月至1918年3月陈望道（注册姓名陈参一）就读于日本东洋大学印度哲学伦理学科

▲ 1919年7月陈望道毕业于日本中央大学获法学学士学位

宣言中译　信仰之源

「中译：承译巨著　传播火种」
TRANSLATING *THE COMMUNIST MANIFESTO*, SPREADING THE TRUTH OF MARXISM

● 钢笔画《真理的味道》（作者：杨宏福）

宣言中译　信仰之源

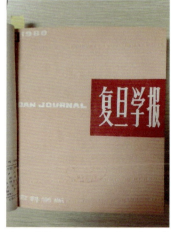

▲ 刊载于1980年第3期《复旦学报（社会科学版）》上的文章《关于上海马克思主义研究会活动的回忆——陈望道同志生前谈话纪录》

• "这次查办斗争（引者按'一师风潮'）使我更加认识所谓除旧布新并不是不推自倒、不招自来的轻而易举的事情。我也就在这次事件的锻炼和启发下，在事件结束之后，回到我的故乡浙江义乌分水塘村去，进修马克思主义，并且试译《共产党宣言》。"

——陈望道

• "The investigation of revolutionary actions ('Zhejiang No. 1 Teachers College Incident') this time made me realize more profoundly that the process of discarding the old and setting up the new is not something that will easily happen on its own. Toughened and inspired by this incident, I returned to my hometown Fen Shui Tang village in Yiwu, Zhejiang, to study Marxism and to try my hand at translating *The Communist Manifesto*".

–Chen Wangdao

宣言中译　信仰之源

1920年至1938年间，《共产党宣言》陈望道译本被先后印刷17次

中共一大会址纪念馆珍藏
1920年8月版　　中共一大会址纪念馆珍藏
1920年9月版

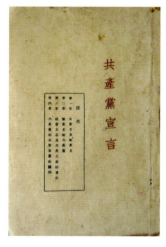
中共一大会址纪念馆珍藏
1924年6月版

北京红展马克思展厅珍藏
1924年9月版

中共一大会址纪念馆珍藏
1925年4月版

中共一大会址纪念馆珍藏
1925年7月版

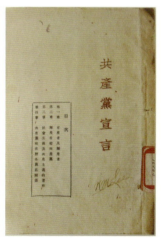
中国国家博物馆珍藏
1926年1月版

宣言中译　信仰之源

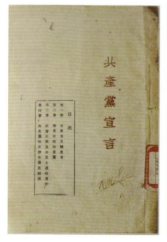
中国国家博物馆珍藏
1926年2月版

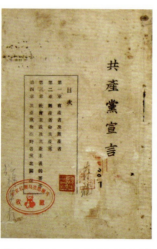
北京红展马克思展厅珍藏
1926年4月版

中共一大会址纪念馆、
复旦大学图书馆珍藏
1926年5月版

复旦大学图书馆珍藏
1927年1月版

中共一大会址纪念馆珍藏
1927年3月版

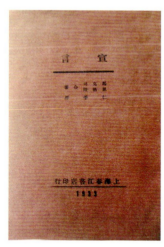
中共一大会址纪念馆珍藏
1933年2月版

北京红展马克思展厅珍藏
1937年11月版

中共中央编译局图书馆珍藏
1938年1月版

北京红展马克思展厅珍藏
1938年版

中共一大会址纪念馆珍藏
1937—1938年版

宣言中译　信仰之源

▲ 《社会主义研究》（20世纪初日本宣传共产主义思潮的小册子，刊有幸德秋水翻译的《共产党宣言》日文译本全文），1961年劳动运动史研究会依据史料重编合订本，系珍贵版本。

◀《共产党宣言》1915年英文版（该版旧书内藏有20世纪20年代中国华西大学图书馆借书卡，系当时中国通行的英文版《共产党宣言》版本，北京大学图书馆也藏有该版本）。陈望道翻译《共产党宣言》依据幸德秋水的日文译本，并依据英文版修正补充。

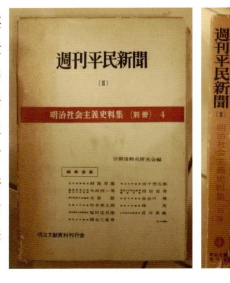

◀《平民新闻》（20世纪初日本宣传共产主义思潮的报纸，刊有节译的《共产党宣言》日文译本），1961年劳动运动史研究会依据史料重编合订本，系珍贵版本。

宣言中译　信仰之源

▲ 完成《共产党宣言》翻译后，陈望道在外国语学社、平民女校担任教员，讲授《共产党宣言》和写作等课程。

▲ 1920年8月，陈望道参与《劳动界》创刊。

◀ 1920年9月，《共产党宣言》出版后，陈望道到复旦任教，图为1920年《复旦年刊》中的教员图录。

宣言中译　信仰之源

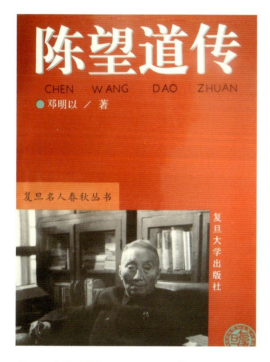

▲《陈望道传》，邓明以著，复旦大学出版社1995年出版。邓明以是陈望道的学生、秘书。传记史料充实，较完整地记录了陈望道的生平事迹，是设展的重要内容依据。

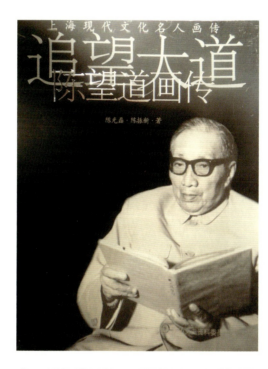

▲《陈望道画传》，陈光磊、陈振新著，上海书店出版社、复旦大学出版社2005年联合出版。陈光磊系陈望道带的研究生，陈振新系陈望道之子。画传收录了作者珍藏与收集的珍贵照片，是设展的重要内容依据。

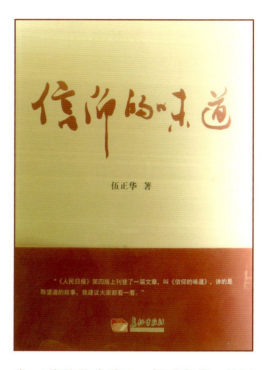

▲《信仰的味道》，伍正华著，长征出版社2016年出版。其中，《信仰的味道》一文，曾受到中共中央总书记、国家主席、中央军委主席习近平的多次表扬，他"建议大家都看一看"。

「影响：信仰之源 时代担当」
FAITH: SPREADING THE TRUTH OF MARXISM, WORKING HARD FOR THE NATION

• "陈译本"《共产党宣言》是用中文刊行的第一本完整的马克思主义经典著作，堪称我国马克思主义经典著作编译史上的一个标志性成果，为中国共产党的诞生作了思想上和理论上的准备。

• Chen Wangdao's translation of *The Communist Manifesto* is the first complete Marxist classic ever published in Chinese, and it can be viewed as a landmark achievement in the translation history of Marxist classics in China. This version prepared for the establishment of the Communist Party of China both ideologically and theoretically.

• 我们重温《共产党宣言》，就是要深刻感悟和把握马克思主义真理力量，坚定马克思主义信仰，追溯马克思主义政党保持先进性和纯洁性的理论源头，提高全党运用马克思主义基本原理解决当代中国实际问题的能力和水平，把《共产党宣言》蕴含的科学原理和科学精神运用到统揽伟大斗争、伟大工程、伟大事业、伟大梦想的实践中去，不断谱写新时代坚持和发展中国特色社会主义新篇章。

——习近平

• When we read *The Communist Manifesto* again, we should deeply appreciate and grasp the power of truth in Marxism, put greater faith in Marxist beliefs, trace the theoretical fountain of the advance and purity of Marxist parties, improve our ability in applying the fundamental theories of Marxism into solving the practical problems in contemporary China. Through the adoption of the scientific theories implied in *The Communist Manifesto* in pushing forward our great cause and realizing our great dream, we can achieve great success in developing our great nation.

–Xi Jinping

宣言中译　信仰之源

- 1936年，毛泽东在陕甘宁边区接受美国记者斯诺采访时曾说："有三本书特别深刻地铭记在我的心中，建立起我对马克思主义的信仰。我接受马克思主义并认为它是对历史的正确解释以后，就一直没有动摇过。这三本书是：《共产党宣言》，陈望道译，这是用中文出版的第一本马克思主义的书……到1920年夏天，在理论上，而且在某种程度的行动上，我已成为一个马克思主义者了。"

- In 1936, Mao Zedong was interviewed by the American journalist Edgar Snow in the Shaanxi-Gansu Border Area. In the interview, he said, "There are three books that have profoundly influenced me and strengthened my belief in Marxism. Since I embrace Marxism and the belief that it is the correct explanation of history, my beliefs have never wavered. These three books are *The Communist Manifesto* translated by Chen Wangdao – the first Marxist book published in Chinese ... In the summer of 1920, I became a Marxist in theory and to a certain extent in practice."

- 1919年周恩来在日本留学时，通过河上肇创办的《社会问题研究》了解《共产党宣言》一书，开始接触马克思主义。1920年10月赴法国留学，和蔡和森等人一起继续学习《共产党宣言》，最终成为共产主义者。1921年，周恩来等在巴黎酝酿成立了社会主义青年团，次年7月改组为中共旅欧总支部，总支部先后出版了《少年》《赤光》等刊物，宣传马克思主义，也宣传《共产党宣言》。

- In 1919 when Zhou Enlai was studying in Japan, he learned about *The Communist Manifesto* and communism through the journal *Studies of Social Problems* edited by Hajime Kawakami. In October 1920, he went to study in France, and continued his study of *The Manifesto* with Cai Hesen and others, and eventually became a communist. In 1921, Zhou Enlai and others established the Socialist Youth League of China in Paris, which became the European branch of the Communist Party of China in the following year. It published periodicals such as *La Jeunesse* and *Lumiere Rouge* to promote Marxism and *The Manifesto*.

宣言中译　信仰之源

- 刘少奇于1920年在上海外国语学社学习时接触到《共产党宣言》。《宣言》的课程就是由刚完成全文翻译的陈望道讲授的。在同学眼里，"看见他（刘少奇）的时候，多是在学习俄文、阅读《宣言》、思考着中国革命的问题"。后来在莫斯科留学期间，他把《宣言》看了又看，从书中了解共产党是干什么的，是怎样的党，他是否准备献身于这个党所从事的事业。经过深思熟虑，他最后决定加入共产党，并献身于党的事业。

- In 1920, Liu Shaoqi learned about *The Communist Manifesto* when studying at Shanghai Foreign Language Society. Chen Wangdao, who had just completed the translation of the book, taught The Manifesto there. His classmates recalled: "When we saw him (Liu Shaoqi), he was mostly studying Russian, reading *The Communist Manifesto* and thinking about the problems of Chinese revolutions." Later, when he was studying in Moscow, he read The Manifesto over and over again. From the book, he comprehended what communism was for, what kind of party it was, and pondered whether he would contribute to the cause of this party. After deep consideration, he finally decided to join the Communist Party and devote himself to the party's cause.

宣言中译　信仰之源

- 朱德于1922年10月抵德国，读到了《共产党宣言》。他曾回忆："(1921年前)，我们连一份《共产党宣言》都没有，那是最早翻译成中文的马克思主义文献。……（1922年11月，朱德由周恩来介绍入党后，加入柏林支部）研究和讨论了已经译成中文的马克思主义文献《共产党宣言》和共产主义的入门书。……我在德国研究马克思列宁主义的书籍，参加了中国共产党，从此开始走上了新的革命旅程。"

- In October 1922, Zhu De arrived in Germany, and came across *The Communist Manifesto*. He once recalled: "(Before 1921), we did not even have a copy of *The Communist Manifesto*, and it was the earliest Marxist work translated into Chinese ... (In November 1921, on Zhou Enlai's recommendation, Zhu De joined the Berlin branch of the Communist Party) I studied and talked about *The Manifesto* and other communist books, which was already translated into Chinese. ... I studied books on Marxism-Leninism in Germany, joined the Chinese Communist Party, and from then on embarked on a new revolutionary journey."

宣言中译　信仰之源

• 邓小平于1992年在武昌、深圳、珠海、上海等地的谈话中曾说过："学马列要精，要管用的。……我的入门老师是《共产党宣言》和《共产主义ABC》。……马克思主义的真理颠扑不破。实事求是是马克思主义的精髓。……其实马克思主义并不玄奥。马克思主义是很朴实的东西，很朴实的道理。我坚信，世界上赞成马克思主义的人会多起来的，因为马克思主义是科学。它运用历史唯物主义揭示了人类社会发展的规律。"

• In 1992, Deng Xiaoping mentioned in the several speeches he gave in Wuchang, Shenzhen, Zhuhai and Shanghai that "It is necessary to accurately understand and properly apply Marxism-Leninism. ... My guides are *The Communist Manifesto* and *The ABC of Communism* ... The truth of Marxism is irrefutable. Realism is the essence of Marxism. ... Marxism is indeed not abstruse. It is something that is simple and clear, and it is a theory that is understandable. I strongly believe that an increasing number of people will agree with Marxism because Marxism is a science. It uses historical materialism to reveal the pattern of the development human society."

- 1970年12月14日，陈云给二女儿陈伟华的信中说："学习马列主义、增加革命知识，不能单靠几篇哲学著作。……我认为你应该这样学。一、订一份《参考消息》。……二、每天看报。最好看《人民日报》……三、找一本《中国近代史》看看（从鸦片战争到解放）……四、找一本世界革命史看看。……五、马克思、恩格斯、列宁的著作很多，但我看来，只要十本到十五本就可以了。（一）《共产党宣言》是必须看的。……"

- Chen Yun remarked in his letter to his second daughter Chen Weihua on December 14, 1970, "Learning Marxism-Leninism and acquiring further revolutionary knowledge cannot rely on only certain famous philosophical works. ... I think you should learn it this way: 1. subscribe to *Reference News* ... 2. read newspapers every day, preferably *People Daily* ... 3. find and read *Modern History of China* (From the Opium War to the War of Liberation) ... 4. find and read a book on the global history of revolution ... 5. Marx, Engels, and Lenin published many works, but in my opinion, ten to fifteen volumes of them are sufficient. *The Communist Manifesto* is a must - read."

宣言中译　信仰之源

• 1996年，江泽民在中央党校的一次讲话中回忆到，他在上海交通大学读书时，曾在晚上打着手电筒读《共产党宣言》。2001年，他在"七一"讲话中指出："马克思主义不是教条，只有正确运用于实践并在实践中不断发展才具有强大的生命力。"这是对待马克思主义的科学态度。马克思、恩格斯在为《共产党宣言》所作的七个序言中，就突出强调了这种科学态度。

• In 1996, Jiang Zemin recalled in a talk at the Central Party School that when he studied at Shanghai Jiaotong University, he used to read *The Communist Manifesto* at night with a torch. In 2001, he pointed out in the "July 1" speech that "Marxism is not a doctrine, and it will only show strong vitality when it is correctly applied to practice and developed in practice." This is the scientific attitude that should be adopted towards Marxism. Marx and Engels emphasized this scientific attitude in the seven prefaces to *The Manifesto*.

- 2007年，胡锦涛在党的十七大报告中指出："《共产党宣言》发表以来近一百六十年的实践证明，马克思主义只有与本国国情相结合、与时代发展同进步、与人民群众共命运，才能焕发出强大的生命力、创造力、感召力。"他也多次要求全党同志特别是党的各级领导干部，要坚定理想信念，增强为党和人民事业不懈奋斗的自觉性和坚定性，咬定青山不放松。

- In 2007, Hu Jintao stated in the 17th National Congress of the Communist Party of China, "Practices since the publication of *The Communist Manifesto* nearly 160 years ago have proved that only when Marxism is integrated with the conditions of a specific country, in step with the advances of the times and tied to the destiny of the people can it demonstrate its strong vitality, creativity, and appeal." He also called on all Party members several times, especially the leading cadres at all levels, to commit to their ideal and belief, and to strengthen their consciousness and determination to make unremitting efforts for the national cause.

宣言中译　信仰之源

不忘初心　REMAINING TRUE TO OUR ORIGINAL ASPIRATION

「不忘初心 牢记使命」
REMAINING TRUE TO OUR ORIGINAL ASPIRATION AND KEEPING OUR MISSION FIRMLY IN MIND

- 不忘初心，方得始终。中国共产党人的初心和使命，就是为中国人民谋幸福，为中华民族谋复兴。这个初心和使命是激励中国共产党人不断前进的根本动力。

- Never forget why you started, and you can accomplish your mission. The original aspiration and mission of the members of the Chinese Communist Party are working for the happiness of the Chinese people and the rejuvenation of the Chinese nation. The original aspiration and mission are the fundamental forces that drive the Chinese Communist Party to forge ahead.

宣言中译　信仰之源

真理的味道
TASTE OF TRUTH

- 1920年的春夜，浙江义乌分水塘村一间久未修葺的柴屋。两张长凳架起一块木板，既是床铺，又是书桌。桌前，有一个人在奋笔疾书。

- 母亲在屋外喊："红糖够不够，要不要我再给你添些？"儿子应声答道："够甜，够甜的了！"谁知，当母亲进来收拾碗筷时，却发现儿子的嘴里满是墨汁，红糖却一点儿也没动。原来，儿子竟然是蘸着墨汁吃掉粽子的!

- 他叫陈望道，他翻译的册子叫《共产党宣言》。

- 习近平总书记曾多次援引这则故事：

- 墨汁为什么那样甜？原来，真理也是有味道的，甚至比红糖更甜。正因为这种无以言喻的精神之甘、信仰之甜，无数的革命先辈才情愿吃百般苦、甘心受千般难。

- One night in the spring of 1920, in a crude deserted room at Fenshuitang village in Yiwu, Zhejiang, a man was working hard. He had been reading and writing day and night, by two benches, doubling as a desk or a bed.

- His mother called from outside the room: "Is the brown sugar enough for you? Do you need more?" He replied, "That's enough as it's very sweet!"

- Surprisingly, when his mother came inside to clean up the dishes later, she found that her son's mouth was full of ink and the brown sugar remained untouched. It turned out that her son had actually eaten the zongzi dipped in ink!

- The man was Chen Wangdao, and what he was translating was *The Communist Manifesto*.

- President Xi Jinping has repeatedly mentioned this story, for it is a story about truth.

宣言中译　信仰之源

- 现通行英文版
- 日文（幸德秋水译）版
- **中文（陈望道译）版**
- 现通行中文版

- A spectre is haunting Europe – the spectre of communism.
- 一個の怪物歐洲を徘徊す。共產主義の怪物是れ也。
- **有一個怪物，在歐洲徘徊著，這怪物就是共產主義。**
- 一个幽灵，共产主义的幽灵，在欧洲游荡。

- What the bourgeoisie therefore produces, above all, are its own grave-diggers. Its fall and the victory of the proletariat are equally inevitable.
- 故に紳士閥が產出する所の者は、第一に自己の墓堀なり。其沒落と平民の勝利とは共に避く可らざるの事たり。
- **有產階級所造成的，首先就是自己的墳墓。有產階級底傾覆和無產階級底勝利，都是免不了的事。**
- 它首先生产的是它自身的掘墓人。资产阶级的灭亡和无产阶级的胜利是同样不可避免的。

- We shall have an association, in which the free development of each is the condition for the free development of all.
- 之に代ふるに、各人自由に發達すれば萬人亦從つて自由に發達するが如き、協同社會を以てせんと欲するなり。
- **換上各個人都能夠自由發達，全體才能夠自由發達的協同社會。**
- 代替那存在着阶级和阶级对立的资产阶级旧社会的，将是这样一个联合体，在那里，每个人的自由发展是一切人的自由发展的条件。

- The proletarians have nothing to lose but their chains. They have a world to win
- 勞働者の失ふべき所は唯だ鐵鎖のみ。而して其の得る所は全世界なり。
- **無產階級所失的不過是他們的鎖鏈，得到的是全世界。**
- 无产者在这个革命中失去的只是锁链。他们获得的将是整个世界。

- Working Men of All Countries, Unite!
- 萬國の勞働者團結せよ！
- **万国劳动者团结起来呵！**
- 全世界无产者，联合起来！

宣言中译　信仰之源

YOUXIN PRESS　又新出版

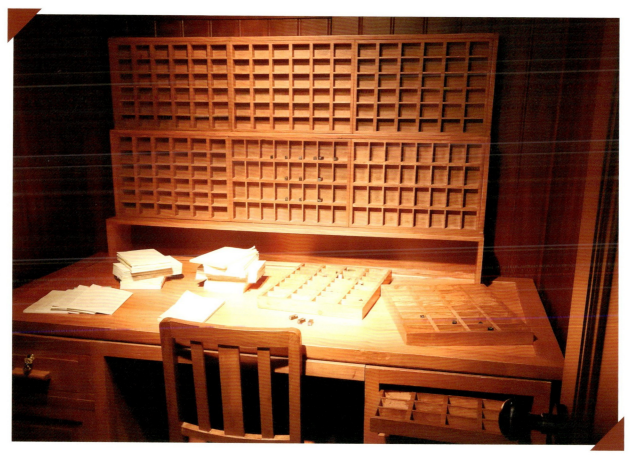

● 又新印刷所场景再现

宣言中译　信仰之源

◀ 该书初版1000册。封面红印马克思半身肖像，肖像下面自右向左横题"马格斯"三字；肖像上面大字横题书名"共党产宣言"。还印着几行小字：社会主义研究小丛书第一辑，马格斯、安格尔斯合著，陈望道译。书末版权页上还印着：一千九百二十年八月出版；印刷及发行者：社会主义研究社；定价大洋一角。该书为竖排平装本，用5号铅字排印，报纸印造。由于排印疏忽，封面上的"共产党宣言"印成了"共党产宣言"。全书共56页，32开。1920年9月，《共产党宣言》重印1000册。1920—1938年间，陈望道译本被先后印制了17次。

▲ 1975年1月，陈望道去北京图书馆（现为国家图书馆）参观，副馆长鲍正鹄（陈望道学生，毕业于复旦大学中文系）取出该馆珍藏的1920年9月版《共产党宣言》，特请译者陈望道签名纪念。

▲ 1920年8月，第一本《共产党宣言》中文全译本终于问世，由秘密成立的又新印刷所（在上海拉斐德路即今复兴中路成裕里12号）承印。

宣言中译　信仰之源

THE COMMUNIST MANIFESTO COLLECTIONS 版本阅读

● 版本厅

宣言中译　信仰之源

馆藏《共产党宣言》版本清单

语种	出版时间	语种	出版时间
中文	1948年，百周年纪念版	中文	1964年9月第6版，1967年3月北京第1次印刷
中文	1948年	中文	1964年9月第6版，1967年8月黑龙江第1次印刷
中文	1949年，干部必读版	中文	1964年9月第6版，1970年12月北京第21次印刷
中文	1949年，百周年纪念版	中文	1964年9月第6版，1971年3月河南第1次印刷
中文	1951年10月第4版，1954年3月沈阳第6次印刷	中文	1964年9月第6版，1971年4月河北第1次印刷
中文	1951年10月第4版，1955年1月北京第8次印刷	中文	1964年9月第6版，1971年4月山西第2次印刷
中文	1951年10月第4版，1956年6月北京第10次印刷	中文	1964年9月第6版，1971年4月四川第1次印刷
中文	1959年8月第5版，1959年11月上海第11次印刷	中文	1964年9月第6版，1971年4月湖北第4次印刷
中文	1959年9月第6版，1961年11月北京第17次印刷	中文	1964年9月第6版，1971年5月江苏第1次印刷
中文	1964年9月第6版，1964年12月武汉第3次印刷	中文	1964年9月第6版，1971年7月吉林第6次印刷
中文	1964年9月第6版，1966年2月北京第20次印刷	中文	1964年9月第6版，1971年8月北京第22次印刷

语种	出版时间	语种	出版时间
中文	1964年9月第6版，1972年4月天津第5次印刷	中文	1956年
中文	1964年9月第6版，1972年4月哈尔滨第5次印刷	中文	1958年，汉语拼音注音版
中文	1964年9月第6版，1973年3月江苏第7次印刷	中文	据1959年8月第5版重排，1963年4月北京第1次印刷
中文	1964年9月第6版，1973年3月湖北第8次印刷	中文	1960年
中文	1964年9月第6版，1973年4月山西第4次印刷	中文	1962年
中文	1964年9月第6版，1973年8月山西第5次印刷	中文	1963年
中文	1964年9月第6版，1974年1月北京第25次印刷	中文	据1964年9月第6版重排，1970年12月北京第2次印刷
中文	1964年9月第6版，1974年10月浙江第11次印刷	中文	1968年
中文	1964年9月第6版，1975年1月吉林第7次印刷	中文	1968年，云南大学《共产党宣言》杂志编辑部
中文	1964年9月第6版，1976年1月上海第18次印刷	中文	1972年，中国人民解放军战士出版社翻印
中文	1949年12月北京初版，1953年3月北京4版	中文	据1974年第6版重排，1975年4月兰州第1次印刷
中文	1950年	中文	据1974年第6版重排，1975年4月南京第1次印刷
中文	1950年莫斯科，外国文书籍出版局	中文	1977年，未定稿版

宣言中译　信仰之源

语种	出版时间	语种	出版时间
中文	1978年，首版《共产党宣言》纪念版	中文	2011年，彩图注释版
中文	1989年	中文	2012年，图典
中文	1990年	中文	2012年，汉译图典
中文	1991年第2版，1991年9月河南第1次印刷	中文	2014年12月第1版，2015年5月北京第2次印刷
中文	1991年	中文	2014年12月第1版，2015年9月北京第3次印刷
中文	1992年	中文	2014年12月第1版，2017年8月北京第8次印刷
中文	1992年第2版，1992年3月北京第1次印刷	中文	2015年
中文	1992年1月第1版，1992年1月第1次印刷《共产党宣言》导读	中文	线装版
中文	1997年，画说版	中文	编译局译本
中文	1997年	盲文	1971年
中文	1998年第1版，1册1函套，中央编译出版社	维吾尔文	1971年
中文	1998年第1版，1999年2月第2次印刷 外语教学与研究出版社	藏文	1971年
中文	2005年	中英对照	1949年之前，具体时间不详

语种	出版时间	语种	出版时间
俄汉对照	1950年	德文	1931年，北京红展马克思展厅赠送，56页
俄汉对照	1950年，北京红展马克思展厅赠送，111页	德文	1931年，北京红展马克思展厅赠送，100页
俄汉对照	1954年	德文	1945年，北京红展马克思展厅赠送，56页
俄汉对照	1954年，北京红展马克思展厅赠送，185页	德文	1945年，北京红展马克思展厅赠送，32页
世界语	1938年	德文	1945年，北京红展马克思展厅赠送，47页
世界语	1948年，北京红展马克思展厅赠送，60页	德文	1945年，北京红展马克思展厅赠送，75页
世界语	具体时间不详，北京红展马克思展厅赠送，60页	德文	1945年，北京红展马克思展厅赠送，65页
德文	1848年，首版《共产党宣言》1978年纪念版	德文	1946年，北京红展马克思展厅赠送，64页
德文	1891年，北京红展马克思展厅赠送，32页	德文	1946年，北京红展马克思展厅赠送，67页
德文	1918年，北京红展马克思展厅赠送，56页	德文	1946年，北京红展马克思展厅赠送，51页
德文	1919年，北京红展马克思展厅赠送，55页	德文	1946年，北京红展马克思展厅赠送，71页
德文	1923年，北京红展马克思展厅赠送，71页	德文	1946年，北京红展马克思展厅赠送，32页
德文	1930年，北京红展马克思展厅赠送，56页	德文	1947年，北京红展马克思展厅赠送，63页

宣言中译　信仰之源

语种	出版时间	语种	出版时间
德文	1931年，北京红展马克思展厅赠送，56页	德文	1948年，北京红展马克思展厅赠送，80页
德文	1931年，北京红展马克思展厅赠送，100页	德文	1952年，北京红展马克思展厅赠送，54页
德文	1945年，北京红展马克思展厅赠送，56页	德文	1953年，北京红展马克思展厅赠送，89页
德文	1945年，北京红展马克思展厅赠送，32页	德文	1959年，北京红展马克思展厅赠送，89页
德文	1945年，北京红展马克思展厅赠送，47页	德文	1964年，北京红展马克思展厅赠送，112页
德文	1945年，北京红展马克思展厅赠送，75页	德文	1965年，北京红展马克思展厅赠送，84页
德文	1945年，北京红展马克思展厅赠送，65页	德文	1968年，北京红展马克思展厅赠送，112页
德文	1946年，北京红展马克思展厅赠送，64页	德文	1970年，北京红展马克思展厅赠送，108页
德文	1946年，北京红展马克思展厅赠送，67页	德文	1972年，北京红展马克思展厅赠送，356页
德文	1946年，北京红展马克思展厅赠送，51页	德文	1973年，北京红展马克思展厅赠送，311页
德文	1946年，北京红展马克思展厅赠送，71页	德文	1973年，北京红展马克思展厅赠送，267页
德文	1946年，北京红展马克思展厅赠送，32页	德文	1975年，北京红展马克思展厅赠送，151页
德文	1947年，北京红展马克思展厅赠送，63页	德文	1975年，注释版

语种	出版时间	语种	出版时间
德文	1987年，北京红展马克思展厅赠送，70页	英文	1939年，北京红展马克思展厅赠送，48页
德文	2003年，北京红展马克思展厅赠送，23页	英文	1946年，北京红展马克思展厅赠送，58页
德文	2005年，北京红展马克思展厅赠送，137页	英文	1947年，北京红展马克思展厅赠送，64页
德文	2009年，北京红展马克思展厅赠送，79页	英文	1948年，百周年纪念版，北京红展马克思展厅赠送，30页
德文	2012年，北京红展马克思展厅赠送，79页	英文	1948年，北京红展马克思展厅赠送，96页
德文	时间不详，北京红展马克思展厅赠送，64页	英文	1948年，北京红展马克思展厅赠送，168页
德文	时间不详，北京红展马克思展厅赠送，54页	英文	1948年，北京红展马克思展厅赠送，48页
英文	1888年，北京红展马克思展厅赠送，31页	英文	1948年，北京红展马克思展厅赠送，64页
英文	1915年	英文	1954年，北京红展马克思展厅赠送，82页
英文	1932年，北京红展马克思展厅赠送 第320~355页为宣言文本	英文	1955年，北京红展马克思展厅赠送，120页
英文	1934年，北京红展马克思展厅赠送，48页	英文	1955年，北京红展马克思展厅赠送，96页
英文	1935年，北京红展马克思展厅赠送，47页	英文	1960年，北京红展马克思展厅赠送，108页
英文	1937年，北京红展马克思展厅赠送，48页	英文	1965年，北京红展马克思展厅赠送，82页

宣言中译　信仰之源

语种	出版时间	语种	出版时间
英文	1965年第1版，1972年第4次印刷	英文	2008年，北京红展马克思展厅赠送，52页
英文	1968年，北京红展马克思展厅赠送，83页	英文	2008年，北京红展马克思展厅赠送，68页
英文	1972年，北京红展马克思展厅赠送，84页	英文	2010年，北京红展马克思展厅赠送，108页
英文	1977年，北京红展马克思展厅赠送，96页	英文	2010年，北京红展马克思展厅赠送，70页
英文	1977年，北京红展马克思展厅赠送，83页	英文	2010年，北京红展马克思展厅赠送，94页
英文	1977年，北京红展马克思展厅赠送，106页	英文	2012年，北京红展马克思展厅赠送，30页
英文	1985年，北京红展马克思展厅赠送，121页	英文	2014年，北京红展马克思展厅赠送，31页
英文	1992年，北京红展马克思展厅赠送，48页	英文	2014年，北京红展马克思展厅赠送，56页
英文	1992年，北京红展马克思展厅赠送，68页	英文	2015年，北京红展马克思展厅赠送，95页
英文	1996年，北京红展马克思展厅赠送，55页	英文	2004, Penguin Books
英文	1998年，北京红展马克思展厅赠送，94页	英文	2012, VERSO
英文	1998年，北京红展马克思展厅赠送，62页	英文	2015, Penguin classics
英文	2003年，北京红展马克思展厅赠送，284页	英文	2016, VERSO

语种	出版时间	语种	出版时间
法文	1901年	法文	1977年，北京红展马克思展厅赠送，第17~61页为宣言文本
法文	1901年，北京红展马克思展厅赠送，97页	法文	1987年，北京红展马克思展厅赠送，184页
法文	1944年，北京红展马克思展厅赠送，60页	法文	1994年，北京红展马克思展厅赠送，79页
法文	1945年，北京红展马克思展厅赠送，58页	法文	1997年，北京红展马克思展厅赠送
法文	1945年，北京红展马克思展厅赠送，46页	法文	1998年，北京红展马克思展厅赠送，91页
法文	1948年，北京红展马克思展厅赠送，62页	俄文	1905年，北京红展马克思展厅赠送，88页
法文	1960年，北京红展马克思展厅赠送，78页	俄文	1923年，北京红展马克思展厅赠送，387页
法文	1962年，北京红展马克思展厅赠送，79页	俄文	1939年，北京红展马克思展厅赠送，85页
法文	1970年，北京红展马克思展厅赠送，82页	俄文	1948年，百周年纪念版
法文	1973年，北京红展马克思展厅赠送，110页	俄文	1948年，北京红展马克思展厅赠送，102页
法文	1973年，北京红展马克思展厅赠送，第5~55页为宣言文本	俄文	1951年，北京红展马克思展厅赠送，71页
法文	1975年	俄文	1952年，北京红展马克思展厅赠送，71页
法文	1977年，北京红展马克思展厅赠送，第31~76页为宣言文本	俄文	1959年，北京红展马克思展厅赠送，71页

宣言中译　信仰之源

语种	出版时间	语种	出版时间
俄文	1960年，北京红展马克思展厅赠送，71页	日文	1945年，北京红展马克思展厅赠送，60页
俄文	1966年，北京红展马克思展厅赠送，123页	日文	昭和二十年（1945年）出版
俄文	1972年，北京红展马克思展厅赠送，63页	日文	1947年，北京红展马克思展厅赠送，178页
俄文	1972年，北京红展马克思展厅赠送，89页	日文	1951年，北京红展马克思展厅赠送，178页
俄文	1972年，32开，第1版	日文	1989年
俄文	1989年，北京红展马克思展厅赠送，63页	弗拉芒文（荷兰）	1917年
西班牙文	1930年	意大利文	1945年，北京红展马克思展厅赠送，54页
西班牙文	1987年，北京红展马克思展厅赠送，61页	意大利文	1945年，北京红展马克思展厅赠送，95页
西班牙文	2007年，北京红展马克思展厅赠送，125页	意大利文	1948年
西班牙文	2008年，北京红展马克思展厅赠送，125页	意大利文	1948年，北京红展马克思展厅赠送，304页
西班牙文	2011年，北京红展马克思展厅赠送，311页	意大利文	1949年，北京红展马克思展厅赠送，73页
西班牙文	2013年，北京红展马克思展厅赠送，125页	意大利文	1958年，北京红展马克思展厅赠送，136页
西班牙文	2018年，袖珍版	意大利文	1967年，北京红展马克思展厅赠送，93页

语种	出版时间	语种	出版时间
意大利文	1969年，北京红展马克思展厅赠送，123页	意大利文	2008年，北京红展马克思展厅赠送，234页
意大利文	1971年，北京红展马克思展厅赠送，115页	意大利文	2009年，北京红展马克思展厅赠送，157页
意大利文	1971年，北京红展马克思展厅赠送，96页	意大利文	2012年，北京红展马克思展厅赠送，89页
意大利文	1973年，北京红展马克思展厅赠送，91页	意大利文	2013年，北京红展马克思展厅赠送，157页
意大利文	1976年，北京红展马克思展厅赠送，103页	丹麦文	1926年，北京红展马克思展厅赠送，64页
意大利文	1978年，北京红展马克思展厅赠送，330页	丹麦文	1946年，北京红展马克思展厅赠送，62页
意大利文	1983年，北京红展马克思展厅赠送，95页	丹麦文	1971年
意大利文	1992年，北京红展马克思展厅赠送，85页	朝鲜文	1971年
意大利文	1994年，北京红展马克思展厅赠送，95页	捷克文	1945年，内有铅笔阅读划线，北京红展马克思展厅赠送，30页
意大利文	1998年，北京红展马克思展厅赠送，220页	捷克文	1946年
意大利文	1998年，北京红展马克思展厅赠送，67页	捷克文	1946年，北京红展马克思展厅赠送，108页
意大利文	1998年，北京红展马克思展厅赠送，78页	捷克文	1949年，北京红展马克思展厅赠送，78页
意大利文	1999年，北京红展马克思展厅赠送，62页	捷克文	1970年，北京红展马克思展厅赠送

宣言中译　信仰之源

语种	出版时间	语种	出版时间
捷克文	1973年，北京红展马克思展厅赠送，112页	印地文	2008年
波兰文	1907年，北京红展马克思展厅赠送，29页	印地文	2013年
波兰文	1948年，北京红展马克思展厅赠送，98页	印地文	2014年，北京红展马克思展厅赠送，111页
波兰文	1949年	立陶宛语	1976年
波兰文	1956年，北京红展马克思展厅赠送，107页	塞尔维亚文	1945年，北京红展马克思展厅赠送，64页
波兰文	1966年，北京红展马克思展厅赠送，123页	塞尔维亚文	1947年，北京红展马克思展厅赠送，39页
波兰文	1969年，北京红展马克思展厅赠送，131页	塞尔维亚文	1973年，北京红展马克思展厅赠送，220页
波兰文	1976年，北京红展马克思展厅赠送，141页	塞尔维亚文	1977年
爱沙尼亚文	1955年	塞尔维亚文	出版时间不详，北京红展马克思展厅赠送，333页
爱沙尼亚文	1966年，北京红展马克思展厅赠送，71页	布列塔尼语	1978年
乌克兰文	1975年，袖珍版	希腊文	1980年
印尼文	1973年	匈牙利文	1918年，北京红展马克思展厅赠送，67页
印尼文	2015年，北京红展马克思展厅赠送，88页	匈牙利文	1945年，北京红展马克思展厅赠送，33页

语种	出版时间	语种	出版时间
匈牙利文	1948年，有阅读划线，北京红展马克思展厅赠送，59页	瑞典文	1909年，北京红展马克思展厅赠送，44页
匈牙利文	1948年，北京红展马克思展厅赠送，199页	瑞典文	1919年，北京红展马克思展厅赠送，70页
匈牙利文	1948年，北京红展马克思展厅赠送，83页	瑞典文	1948年，北京红展马克思展厅赠送，46页
匈牙利文	1970年，北京红展马克思展厅赠送，130页	瑞典文	1968年，北京红展马克思展厅赠送，75页
匈牙利文	1980年	瑞典文	2014年
爱尔兰文	1986年	马拉雅拉姆语	2015年
毛里求斯克里奥尔语	2005年	马来文	2016年
科西嘉语	2012年	老挝语	2016年，北京红展马克思展厅赠送，72页
泰米尔文	2010年，北京红展马克思展厅赠送，100页	缅甸文	2014年，北京红展马克思展厅赠送，120页
泰米尔文	2012年	冰岛文	1924年，北京红展马克思展厅赠送，75页
泰米尔文	2012年，北京红展马克思展厅赠送，116页	罗马尼亚文	1947年，北京红展马克思展厅赠送，86页
泰卢固语	2015年	罗马尼亚文	1949年，北京红展马克思展厅赠送，95页
泰卢固语	2015年，北京红展马克思展厅赠送，87页	罗马尼亚文	1962年，北京红展马克思展厅赠送，101页

宣言中译　信仰之源

语种	出版时间	语种	出版时间
罗马尼亚文	1998年，北京红展马克思展厅赠送，186页	葡萄牙文	2009年，北京红展马克思展厅赠送，152页
保加利亚文	1944年，北京红展马克思展厅赠送，56页	斯洛文尼亚文	1949年，北京红展马克思展厅赠送，91页
保加利亚文	1948年，北京红展马克思展厅赠送，153页	斯洛伐克文	1950年，北京红展马克思展厅赠送，110页
荷兰文	1917年，北京红展马克思展厅赠送，68页	马耳他文	1982年，北京红展马克思展厅赠送，55页
荷兰文	1935年，北京红展马克思展厅赠送，112页		
荷兰文	1945年，北京红展马克思展厅赠送，40页		
荷兰文	1948年，北京红展马克思展厅赠送，93页		
荷兰文	1968年，北京红展马克思展厅赠送，111页		
土耳其文	2005年，北京红展马克思展厅赠送，71页		
土耳其文	2013年，北京红展马克思展厅赠送，92页		
土耳其文	2014年，北京红展马克思展厅赠送，88页		
葡萄牙文	2006年，北京红展马克思展厅赠送，123页		
葡萄牙文	2006年，北京红展马克思展厅赠送，131页		

― 千秋巨笔　一代宗师 ―

光辉一生　LIFE STORY

● 年表厅（原为旧居藏书室）

出生（1891年）	{	1月18日（光绪十六年腊月初九）出生于浙江省义乌县河里乡分水塘村【图1】
15岁（1906年）	{	入义乌县城绣湖书院学习数学、博物
16岁（1907年）	{	回分水塘村，带领青年破除迷信，兴办村学，招募村童入学
17岁至21岁（1908年至1912年）	{	考入浙江第七中学（金华中学），学习数理化等现代学科知识
22岁至23岁（1913年至1914年）	{	在上海补习学校学习英文 入杭州之江大学学习英文和数学，为出国留学作准备
24岁至27岁（1915年至1918年）	{	赴日本留学。先后在早稻田大学、东京物理学校、东洋大学、中央大学就读 俄国十月革命后，开始接受马克思主义
28岁（1919年）	{	毕业于日本中央大学法科，获法学学士学位 回国后，9月受聘于浙江第一师范学校，任国文教员，宣传新文化、新思想
29岁（1920年）	{	浙江"一师风潮"后，回乡完成《共产党宣言》的翻译【图2】 5月1日偕同陈独秀、施存统在上海澄衷中学发起纪念五一国际劳动节，这是中国工人阶级第一次纪念此节日 5月，与陈独秀、李达、李汉俊等组建马克思主义研究会 8月所译《共产党宣言》出版，接着于9月再版 9月，应聘至复旦大学任教【图3】

【图1】

【图2】

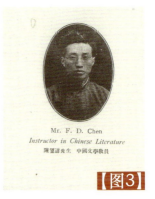
【图3】

30岁（1921年）	中共一大后，受命任中共上海地方委员会第一任书记 主编《民国日报》副刊《妇女评论》（于8月3日创刊），发表创刊宣言 在平民女校任教，讲授作文法；在外国语学社讲授《共产党宣言》
31岁（1922年）	农历正月初一，参加上海党组织上街散发"贺年帖"活动，为贺年帖拟写宣传共产主义的"太平歌" 所撰《作文法讲义》于3月由上海民智书局出版，为第一部有系统的白话作文法著作。
32岁（1923年）	8月，受陈独秀委派，到上海大学任中文系主任
34岁（1925年）	"五卅"运动爆发后，接任上海大学教务长和代理校务主任；起草宣言，发表通电，抗议帝国主义暴行
36岁（1927年）	所撰《美学概论》出版 9月，任复旦大学中文系主任和复旦实验中学校长
37岁（1928年）	9月，与汪馥泉筹建的大江书铺开业
38岁（1929年）	5月，与施存统合译的《社会意识学大纲》（俄国波格丹诺夫原著）由开明书店出版 出任党领导的中华艺术大学校长
39岁（1930年）	9月，与蔡葵成婚【图4】

【图4】

40岁（1931年）	因保护进步学生遭国民党迫害而离开复旦，蛰居沪上写作《修辞学发凡》 所著《因明学》由世界书局出版
41岁（1932年）	所著《修辞学发凡》分上下两册由大江书铺出版【图5】
43岁（1934年）	发起大众语运动，创刊《太白》，首倡刊物用“手头字”（简体字）印行
44岁（1935年）	与胡愈之、叶圣陶等于6月发起、组织中国语言学会；赴广西大学任中文科主任
46岁（1937年）	回上海，参与发起、组织上海文化界抗日联谊会
47岁（1938年）	在地下党创办的抗日夜大学“社会科学讲习所”任教， 讲授“中国文艺思潮”和“中国语文概论”两门课程
48岁（1939年）	与陈鹤琴等主持、举办“中国语文展览会”
49岁至53岁（1940年至1944年）	回复旦大学（重庆北碚）任教【图6】 历任复旦大学训导长、新闻系主任 发起募捐，筹建复旦大学新闻馆，提出“好学力行”为系铭【图7】

【图5】

國立復旦大學聘書 存根
茲敦聘
陳望道先生為本大學文學院中國文學系專任教授兼新聞學系主任
此訂
校長吳南軒
中華民國三十一年八月 一 日
【图6】

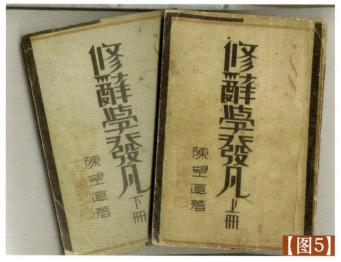

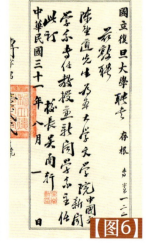

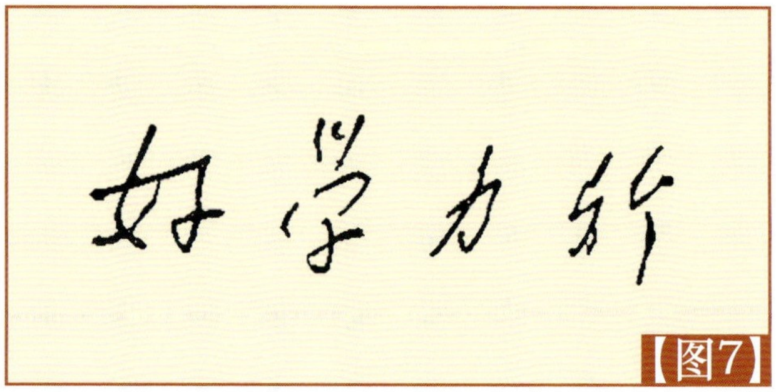

【图7】

54岁（1945年）	和张志让、周谷城等受到在重庆参加国共谈判的毛泽东的邀见
58岁（1949年）	7月，出席第一届中华全国文学艺术工作者代表大会【图8】 受任复旦大学校务委员会副主任兼文学院院长，主持校委会工作 9月，出席政协全国委员会第一次会议 12月，受任华东军政委员会委员
59岁（1950年）	受任华东军政委员会文化教育委员会副主任和文化部部长
60岁（1951年）	6月，加入中国民主同盟
61岁（1952年）	11月，由毛泽东主席签署任命为复旦大学校长【图9】
63岁（1954年）	2月，受任华东行政委员会委员，并任高教局局长 10月，出席中华人民共和国第一届全国人民代表大会
64岁（1955年）	当选中国科学院哲学社会科学部委员【图10】 10月，出席第一次全国文学改革会议和现代汉语规范问题学术讨论会；代表讨论会主席团作总结发言，对确立"普通话"标准的科学表述有所贡献 12月，筹建复旦大学语法、修辞、逻辑研究室（1958年改名为语言研究室）

【图8】

【图9】

【图10】

千秋巨笔 一代宗师

- **65岁（1956年）**
  - 元旦，受到毛泽东主席邀见，毛主席关心其学术研究
  - 上海语文学会于9月成立，为创始会长；被定为一级教授

- **67岁（1958年）**
  - 上海哲学社会科学学会联合会于3月9日成立，当选为社联主席
  - 5月，当选为民盟上海市主任委员；11月，当选为民盟中央副主席

- **70岁（1961年）**
  - 出席上海各界五一劳动节联欢晚会，与毛主席会见谈话 【图11】

- **71岁（1962年）**
  - 3月接任修订《辞海》总主编

- **72岁（1963年）**
  - 3月26日主持召开校务扩大会议，有全体校务委员、全体教师、全体研究生、行政负责人参加，专门讨论学风和校风建设问题；这在复旦校史上是第一次 【图12】

- **82岁（1973年）**
  - 8月，出席中国共产党第十次全国代表大会

- **84岁（1975年）**
  - 当选为第四届全国人大常务委员会委员

- **85岁（1976年）**
  - 在病榻上完成《文法简论》定稿工作

- **86岁（1977年）**
  - 10月29日凌晨4时病逝于华东医院

【图11】

【图12】

千秋巨笔 一代宗师

静穆书房 STORY

● 望道书房（原为旧居书房）

千秋巨笔　一代宗师

▲ 陈望道蜡像实景图

▲ 蜡像服装原件

▲ 蜡像制作参考图和泥塑小样

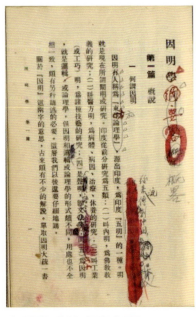

▲ 蜡像手持书稿左页：
《因明学》再版手迹

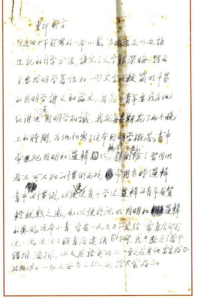

▲ 蜡像手持书稿左页：
《因明学》重印前言

千秋巨笔　一代宗师

▲ 蜡像持笔原件

▲ 1965年5月，陈望道和复旦大学新闻系师生一起欢庆复旦大学创办六十周年。

▲ 书房一角：书柜、藤椅与小茶几（旧居家具）

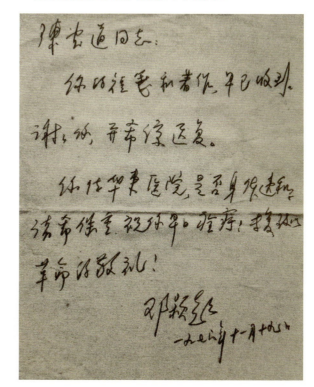

▲ 1976年邓颖超收到再版《修辞学发凡》的回信（仿制件）

▲ 书房一角：
修辞学课程学生记分册
陈望道翻阅过的《市政公报》

▲ 书房一角：
《辞海审查本》《辞海审查本（补遗）》
《辞海审查本附本》《辞海单字表》
《汉语拼音方案在少数民族语地方调查中的应用》
《汉字简化方案草案》

▲ 书房一角：
旋转书柜（旧居家具，原件藏于上海鲁迅纪念馆）

▲ 书房一角：
沙发椅（旧居家具）

千秋巨笔　一代宗师

睹物思人　CLUE OF MEMORY

• 陈望道（1891.1.18-1977.10.29），浙江义乌人，原名参一，又名融，字任重，笔名佛突、雪帆等。首个《共产党宣言》中文全译本的翻译者，中国共产党最早成员之一，著名学者、翻译家、教育家、社会活动家。早年投身新文化运动和宣传共产主义思想的革命活动，1920年5月和陈独秀、李汉俊等人在上海组织马克思主义研究会，6月参与建立上海共产党早期组织，8月出版首个《共产党宣言》中文全译本，同时发起创立中国社会主义青年团。应邀编辑《新青年》，参与创办《劳动界》《共产党》等刊物，并在外国语学社、工人夜校、平民女校授课，为党培养干部。党的一大后，曾任中共上海地方委员会书记。1920年起在复旦大学、上海大学、中华艺术大学等大学任教。1928年创办大江书铺，出版了大量宣传马克思主义的进步书刊。1934年发起"大众语"运动，创办《太白》半月刊。抗日战争时期，参加上海文化界救亡协会等团体的工作，投身抗日爱国运动。1940年辗转去重庆北碚，任复旦大学中文系教授、新闻系主任，支持进步学生的爱国活动。抗战胜利后任华东地区高校教授联合会主任。中华人民共和国成立后，任华东军政委员会文教委员会副主任兼文化部长、复旦大学校长、华东行政委员会高教局长、中科院哲学社会科学部常务委员、《辞海》编委会主编、全国人大和全国政协常委、民盟中央副主席兼上海市主任委员。著有《作文法讲义》《美学概论》《因明学》《修辞学发凡》《文法简论》等。其著述收录于《陈望道文集》（四卷本，上海人民出版社）、《陈望道全集》（十卷本，浙江大学出版社）。

• Chen Wangdao (18 January, 1891 – 29 October, 1977) was born in Yiwu, Zhejiang. He was originally named Canyi and was also known as Rong. His courtesy name is Renzhong, pen names Fotu and Xuefan. He is the translator of the first Chinese version of *The Communist Manifesto*, one of the earliest members of the Communist Party of China, a renowned scholar, translator, educator, and social activist. In his early years, he focused on new-culture revolutionary movements and events in promoting communist ideals. In May 1920, he organized the Shanghai Marxism Research Association with Chen Duxiu, Li Hanjun and others. In June that year, he was involved in the establishment of the early chapter of the Communist Party in Shanghai. In August, his translation of *The Communist Manifesto* was published, and at the same time, he established "the Socialist League of China". He was a guest editor of *The New Youth*, involved in the establishment of *The World of Labour*,

The Communist Party and other publications. He also taught at the Foreign Language Society, the Workers' Night School, the Civilian Girls' School, and educated cadres for the Party. After the first CPC National Congress, he acted as the Secretary of the local chapter of CPC Shanghai. After 1920, he taught at different universities such as Fudan University, Shanghai University, and Chinese University of Arts. In 1928, he established the Dajiang Bookshop which published massive volumes of progressive books and periodicals. In 1934, he started "The Popular Vernacular" movement, established the semimonthly magazine *Tai Bai*. During the War of Resistance Against Japan, he participated in groups such as the salvation association in the cultural circle in Shanghai, and he devoted himself to the patriotic movements against the Japanese invasion. In 1940, after many detours, he went to Beibei, Chongqing to become professor of the Chinese Department at Fudan University and the head of the Journalism Department so as to support the patriotic movements of enlightened students. After the war, he was appointed director of the East China Association of University Professors. After the People's Republic of China was founded, he was appointed deputy head of East China Military and Political Committee, and head of the Culture and Education Commission, president of Fudan University, director of the Administrative Committee of Higher Education. He was also a permanent member of the Philosophy and Social Sciences Department of Chinese Academy of Sciences, head of the editorial board for *Ci Hai*, a member of the standing committee of the National People's Congress and the CPPCC, chairman of China Democratic League in Shanghai, and deputy chairman of China Democratic League. His publications include *Composition Method Lecture*, *An Introduction to Aesthetics*, *Study of Yin Ming*, *Introduction to Rhetoric*, *A Concise Chinese Grammar*, etc. All these works have been included in *The Collected Works of Chen Wangdao* (four volumes, Shanghai People's Press) and *Complete Works of Chen Wangdao* (ten volumes, Zhejiang University Press).

▲ 陈望道站在校园内新闻馆二楼阳台

「破茧」
COCOON-BREAK

● 生平厅之一（原为旧居陈望道卧室）

立志报国 勤奋读书
Studying Hard, Working for the Nation

• 陈望道童年在家乡私塾读四书五经，从人学习拳术。后到义乌县城绣湖书院读书。其间，曾抱着教育救国的志向回村兴办村学，开启民智。在金华府中学堂学习四年后，立志实业救国，并准备留学欧美。1913年先到上海一所补习学校学英语，接着考入杭州之江大学专修英语和数学。后改去日本留学。

• During his childhood, Chen Wangdao used to study the Four Great Books and Five Classics at an old-style private school in his hometown, and also learned traditional Chinese boxing from others. Then, he studied at Xiuhu Academy in the county seat of Yiwu. During that time, he dreamed of going back to the villages to set up schools because of his ideal to save the noction through education. After studying at Jinhua High School for four years, he aspired to seek national salvation through promoting industrial development, and prepared to study overseas in the West. In 1913, he first was admitted into a tutoring school in Shanghai to study English, then Hangchow University where he majored in English and mathematics. Later, he changed his mind and went to study in Japan instead.

▲ 浙江义乌陈宅　　▲ 陈望道的母亲

千秋巨笔 一代宗师

求学东瀛 更名望道
Academic pursuit in Japan, renamed Wangdao

• 1915年，陈望道赴日本留学。先在东京"日华同人共立东亚高等预备学校"进修日语，后在日本早稻田大学法科（1916年9月–1917年5月）、东洋大学印度哲学伦理学科（1917年9月–1918年3月）和中央大学法科就读，其间还在东京物理夜校学习数理课程。最终毕业于中央大学，获法学学士学位。求学期间陈望道参加了反对袁世凯接受日本"二十一条"的卖国条约以及反对洪宪帝制的运动，并开始接触马克思主义，此时他启用"望道"之名，寄寓着向往追求"天下为公"之大道。

• In 1915, Chen Wangdao arrived in Japan to study. He first learned Japanese at the School of Sino-Japan Association and Chinese Overseas Education in Tokyo, then studied law at Waseda University (September 1916 – May 1917), later studied Indian Philosophy and Ethics Theories at Toyo University (September 1917 – March 1918), and finally studied law at Chuo University. During the intervals, he also studied mathematics at Tokyo Science Night School. He eventually graduated from Chuo University and obtained a degree in law. He participated in movements protesting against Yuan Shikai for his accepting "The Twenty-One Demands" treason treaty and movements against Hongxian Monarchy, and came to learn about Marxism during his time in Japan. He used the name of "Wangdao", meaning that he longed for the pursuit of the cause of establishing a "world for the public".

▲ 日本东洋大学学生名册
▲ 刊载《共产党宣言》日文节译文的《平民新闻》
▲ 首次以"望道"署名刊发的文章

一师弄潮 名震四方

Zhejiang No.1 Teachers College Incident – widely known to the public

- 1919年9月，陈望道到浙江第一师范学校任教，与夏丏尊、刘大白、李次九三位国文教员倡导新思想、新文化，大胆改革语文教育，倡导白话文和新文学，被称为"四大金刚"。北洋军阀政府反对新文化运动，视校长经亨颐和教员陈望道为"离经叛道"，以莫须有的罪名加以撤职查办，直至下令解散学校。"一师风潮"促使陈望道经受了一次反抗旧势力斗争的实践考验。

- In September, 1919, Chen Wangdao started to teach at Zhejiang No. 1 Teachers College together with three other Chinese literature instructors, namely Xia Mianzun, Liu Dabai, and Li Cijiu. They inntiated new thouguhts and culture, bravely reformed the languagw education, and initiated vernacular Chinese and new literature – they were known as "The Four Grand Buddha Warrior Attendants". The northern warlords government opposed the rise of new culture movement and viewed Chen Wangdao and the principal Jing Hengyi as the "rebels against orthodoxy". By trumped-up charges the college was demanded to suspend his post until further investigation and the college was eventually disbanded. In "Zhejiang NO. 1 Teacher's College Incident" Chen Wangdao went through a practical test of struggling against the old forces.

▲ "一师风潮"的历史图片
▲ 关于"一师风潮"的报道
▲ 浙江一师出版物《浙潮第一声》

「信仰」
BELIEF

首译宣言 千秋巨笔

Historic influence – the first translator of *The Communist Manifesto*

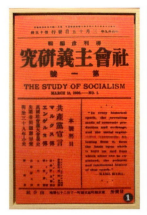 

• "一师风潮"后，经邵力子推荐，陈望道接受《星期评论》社沈玄庐、戴季陶的邀约，回义乌分水塘专心翻译《共产党宣言》。翻译底本为戴季陶提供的日译本和陈独秀从北大图书馆借出的英译本。经过多日的辛勤工作完成了翻译。1920年8月，首个《共产党宣言》中文全译本出版。陈望道在翻译中忘我工作，由于太过投入，以致吃粽子时误蘸墨汁的故事，被传诵为"真理的味道"。

• After "Zhejiang No.1 Teaches College Incident", Chen Wangdao, upon the recommendation of Shao Lizi, accepted the invitation from Shen Xuanlu and Dai Jitao with *Weekly Review* and returned to Fenshuitang Village, Yiwu, to focus on his translation of *The Communist Manifesto*. Dai Jitao provided original copies for the translation which were a Japanese version of *The Communist Manifesto* and an English one which was borrowed from Peking University Library by Chen Duxiu. After months of work, Mr. Chen finished the translation, and in August 1920, the translated version was published. His preoccupation with his translation made him mistakenly dip zongzi into the ink instead of brown sugar while eating it – this story was read as "Taste of Truth".

千秋巨笔　一代宗师

参与建党 开天辟地

Epoch-making: participated in the founding of the Party

• 《共产党宣言》的翻译和出版加速了建党的进程。1920年5月，陈独秀、李汉俊、李达、陈望道等成立"马克思主义研究会"。不久就以"马克思主义研究会"为基础发起建立中国共产党。同时，陈望道也参加组织和建立社会主义青年团，是共青团的创建人之一。

当时报刊上刊登的《上海工人运动宣言》▶

• The translation and publication of *The Communist Manifesto* accelerated the founding of the Communist Party. In May 1920, the Marxist Research Society was established with its core members being Chen Duxiu, Li Hanjun, Li Da, Chen Wangdao, etc. Not long after that, the Communist Party was established on the basis of the Marxist Research Society. At the same time, Chen Wangdao also participated in organizing and establishing the Shanghai Socialist Youth league, and was one of its early founders.

▲《共产党宣言》出版广告

▲ 1922年党内马克思主义读物

组织工作 卓越功绩
Keep Promoting Marxism

- 1920年12月，陈独秀去广东主持教育工作，委托陈望道主持《新青年》编务。陈望道积极开展工作，深入宣传马克思主义，不断扩大《新青年》的影响。1920年8月，陈望道参与了《劳动界》的创刊。1920年11月，参加了《共产党》月刊的创刊。1921年11月间，遵照中国共产党中央局的指示，上海成立了中共上海地方委员会，陈望道为第一任书记。陈望道还曾担任早期党组织的劳工部长，筹建了上海机器工会、印刷工会以及纺织、邮电工会。

◀ 陈望道曾参与《新青年》编务

- In December 1920, when Chen Duxiu went to Guangdong to take charge of educational work, he entrusted Chen Wangdao with the editorial work of *The New Youth*. Chen Wangdao was actively involved in the work through promoting Marxism in depth and continuously expanding the influence of the magazine. In November 1920, he participated in the launching of *Labor* and the monthly magazine *The Communist Party*. One year later, complying with orders of the CPC Central Bureau, the local chapter of the CPC Shanghai was estanlished and Chen Wangdao became its first Sectetary. He also served as the labor minister of the early Communist Party organisations and set up the Shanghai Machine Stotrade, the Printing Union and the Textile, Post and Telecommunications Union.

▲ 陈望道撰写的《太平歌》

— 千秋巨笔　一代宗师 —

❶ 陈望道的记事本

❷ 日记本中夹着陈望道的党费收据条

❸ 陈望道在华东医院

❹ 陈望道在旧居院子听广播

❺ 陈望道生前使用过的物品：钥匙包、钢笔、台灯、收音机、签名印套件、眼镜、放大镜

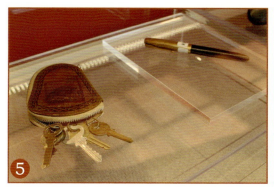

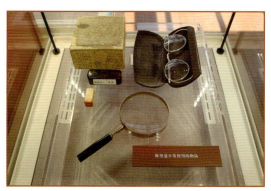

IMPRINT ON FUDAN 复旦印记

「薪火」 LEGACY

● 生平厅之二（原为旧居卧室）

千秋巨笔　一代宗师

红色讲坛 培育火种
Red Forum, kindling the tinder

• 1920年，陈望道在外国语学社讲授《共产党宣言》，并在沪西小沙渡路开办职工补习夜校，亲自上课和演讲。1921年8月，他主编的《民国日报》副刊《妇女评论》创刊。12月，在平民女校任教。1923年秋季，陈望道接受陈独秀的委派，到上海大学工作，任中国文学系主任，后代理校务主任兼教务长。1927年"四一二"反革命政变之后，学校被迫关闭。1929年到由党领导的中华艺术大学主持工作，1930年5月24日该校被反动当局查封。陈望道在这些学校为中国革命培养了大批优秀人才。

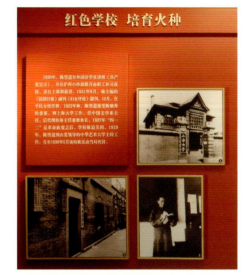

• In 1920, Chen Wangdao taught *The Communist Manifesto* at the Foreign Language Society, and he also established the Workers' Night School where he taught personally at Xiaoshadu Road in west Shanghai. In August 1921, *Minguo Daily*, with Chen Wangdao as its chief editor, published a supplement, *Women's Review*. In December, he taught at the Civilian Girls' School. In autumn, 1923, Chen Wangdao accepted the appointment of Chen Duxiu to teach at Shanghai University as head of the Chinese language program. He later was the acting director of school affairs and registrar. After the counter-revolutionary coup of April 12, 1927, the school was forced to shut down. In 1929, he presided over the party-led Chinese University of Arts which was closed down by the reactionary authority on May 24, 1930. Chen Wangdao trained a large number of outstanding talents for the Chinese revolution in these schools.

▲ 外国语学社旧址

20世纪40年代陈望道在讲课 ▶

▲ 上海大学旧址

大学教育 播散真知
Back to university　Keep on educating

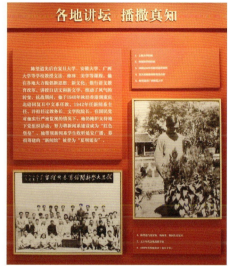

▲ 复旦北碚新闻馆奠基合影

▲ 陈望道在广西师范大学

• 陈望道先后在复旦大学、上海大学、持志大学、安徽大学、广西大学等学校教授文法、修辞、逻辑（论理）、美学等课程。他大力提倡新思想、新文化，推行教育革新。他于1940年秋经香港到重庆北碚，回复旦中文系任教，1942年任新闻系主任，担任过训导长。在国民党对他实行严密监视的情况下，他仍掩护支持地下党组织活动。他发起募捐筹建"新闻馆"，收听延安广播，被誉为"夏坝的延安"。

• Chen Wangdao taught grammar, rhetoric, logic, aesthetics, etc. subsequently at universities such as Fudan University, Shanghai University, Chizhi University, Anhui University, and Guangxi University. He actively encouraged new thoughts, new culture, and education reform. In the autumn of 1940, Mr. Chen returned from Hong Kong to preside over Fudan University which had been relocated to Beibei, Chongqing. In 1942, he became head of the Journalism Department, and the guidance director. Despite the strict monitoring of Kuomintang, he still supported and provided shelter for the actions of the Underground Party. He lanuched a fundraising campaign to build the news library, and journalism students often listened to Yan'an Radio, known as "The Yan'an of Xiaba".

情系复旦 团结服务

Strong Bond with Fudan University: selfless services

- 自1920年9月经邵力子推荐受聘于复旦起，除中间一度被迫离开学校外，陈望道在复旦大学任职近50年。1949年8月1日，陈望道被任命为复旦大学校务委员会副主任兼文学院院长，实际主持学校工作。1952年起任复旦大学校长，直到1977年逝世。1950年到1952年，高校院系进行大调整，全国很多院校、专业合并进复旦，复旦也有部分院系迁出。陈望道胸怀全局，团结来自各地、各界的专家学者，为实现复旦大学的平稳过渡和新的历史性发展做了大量的工作。陈望道为培育复旦优良的校风和学风、为校园建设和规划呕心沥血，深受复旦师生爱戴。

- Upon the recommendation of Shao Lizi to teach at Fudan University in September 1920, Chen Wangdao became a professor at the university and worked there for almost 50 years with the exception of one forced departure. On August 1, 1949, Mr. Chen was appointed deputy director of the university's administrative committee and head of the Faculty of Arts, actually presiding over the university. In 1942, he was appointed president of the university, and remained so till he passed away in 1977. From 1950 to 1952, departments in the university were reformed on a large scale. A lot of colleges and programs from all around the country were incorporated into the university. At the same time, some colleges and programs were removed from the university. Chen Wangdao, with a clear mind, befriended experts and scholars from all around the country, which resulted in the smooth transition and historic growth of Fudan University. Mr. Chen made utmost effort in the cultivation of Fudan's fine school spirit and study style as well as the campus construction and planning, therefore he was beloved and respected by the university's professors and students alike.

▲ 五十年代会见苏联专家

▲ 陈望道与舒文（左一）、陈同生（左二）、夏征农（右二）、杨西光（右一）在复旦

▲ 1959年在校报发表《复旦十年》

「文章」
ACADEMIC WORKS

扬帆奋进 学海领航
The Lighthouse

- 陈望道从事文化教育和学术研究长达60余年，涉猎社会科学的多个领域，在哲学、法学、社会学、伦理学、因明学、美学、文艺学、新闻学等学科均有所成就。主要著作有：《作文法讲义》（1922，民智书局），是"中国有系统的作文法书的第一部"，也是中国第一本白话文的作文法著作；《美学概论》（1927，民智书局），是中国现代美学开创之初极为珍贵的探索；《因明学》（1931，世界书局），是第一本用白话文讲解因明学的著作，更是中国学术史上第一部摆脱佛教玄意，以学理说解因明的论著；《修辞学发凡》（1932，大江书铺），被誉为中国现代修辞学的奠基之作；遗作《文法简论》（1978，上海教育出版社），其所倡导和阐释的语法功能说是20世纪中国语法学最有影响的理论之一，这部著作是他在病榻上完成的，体现了他在学术上生命不息、攀登不止的崇高精神。

- Chen Wangdao engaged in cultural education and academic research for more than 60 years. He engaged widely in various fields of social sciences, and made great achievements in the fields of philosophy, law, sociology, ethics, hetuvidya, aesthetics, literature, journalism, etc. His key works include *Composition Method Lecture* (1922, Intelligence Press), "the first book about the systematic composition method in China" and also the first such book written in vernacular Chinese. *An Introduction to Aesthetics* (1926, Intelligence Press) which was a rare exploration at the early stage of the formation of modern Chinese aesthetics. *Study of Yin Ming* (1930, World Press), the first book in China explaining the thinking tactics of Hetuvidya in vernacular Chinese, also the first book to get rid of Buddhist mysticism and to explore Yin Ming theoretically in Chinese academic history. *Introduction to Rhetoric* (1932, Dajiang Bookstore), known as the foundation which established China's first modern rhetoric system. His posthumous work *A Concise Chinese Grammar* (1978, Shanghai Education Press), the grammatical function advocated and expounded by which is said to be one of the most influential theories of Chinese grammar in the 20th century, and which he finished on sickbed, reflecting his unceasing academic pursuit.

《作文法讲义》

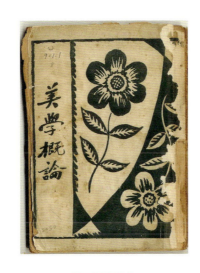
《美学概论》

《因明学纲要》

《修辞学发凡》

《文法简论》

陈望道的代表作

语文改革 勇立潮头
Language reform　Brave in the forefront

- 陈望道早年提倡白话文,主张使用新式标点。1934年,针对当时出现的"文言复兴"思潮,陈望道与陈子展、胡愈之、乐嗣炳等发起"大众语"运动,为白话文的完全胜利、为民族语言共同化的推进作出了巨大贡献,也为打退和冲破国民党的文化"围剿"立下了不可替代的功劳。1938年,他发起中国文法革新的讨论,积极提倡拉丁化新文字运动,发起成立上海语文学会、上海语文教育学会等进步团体。新中国成立后,为推广普通话、简化汉字、制定和推行《汉语拼音方案》等语文建设工作做出了积极的贡献。20世纪60年代初出任《辞海》修订版总主编。

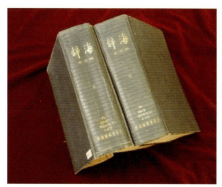

▲ 1962年修订版《辞海》,陈望道任总主编

- In his early years, Chen Wangdao advocated vernacular Chinese and modern punctuations. In 1934, Chen Wangdao, Chen Zizhan, Hu Yuzhi, Yue Sibing and others started the Vernacular Movement aimed at countering trends such as "showing esteem for Confucius and encouraging the reading of classics" and "reviving classical Chinese". This movement made great contributions to the complete victory of vernacular and the communalization of national languages, and also made irreplaceable contributions to repel and break the Kuomingtang cultural "encirclement and suppression". Also it soon became another national enlightenment movement after the May Fourth movement, succeeding in breaking through the "cultural annihilation and suppression" of Kuomintang and popularizing proletarian revolutionary theories. In 1938, he initiated the discussion on the reform of Chinese grammar, actively promoted the movement of adopting Latinised new characters, established progressive groups such as Shanghai Philology Society and Chinese Language Education Society of Shanghai. After the founding of the People's Republic of China, he made active contributions to the construction of languages such as the promotion of Putonghua, the simplification of Chinese characters, and the formulation and implementation of the "Hanyu Pinyin Plan". In 1960s, he became the chief editor of the revised edition of *Ci Hai*.

▲ 陈望道手稿

千秋巨笔　一代宗师

▲ 陈望道剪报

▲ 陈望道手稿

引领学风　实事求是
Promote learning: seeking truth from fact

- 陈望道倡导在学术上采取"古今中外法"，"屁股坐在中国的今天，伸出一只手向古代要东西，伸出另一只手向外国要东西"，"把古的、洋的都'化'在我们的学术研究里面"；"我们的研究有我们自己的样子"。这也是陈望道对自己一生学术经验的总结：融汇古今中外，致力学术创新。在陈望道提议下，1954年起，复旦大学确立了每年举办"校庆科学报告会"的传统，促进了优良学风、校风的形成。

Chen Wangdao advocated the adoption of assimilating from various areas in academic study: sitting in today's China, "on the one hand learn from the ancient times, on the other hand learn from foreign countries", "to incorporate both the ancient and the foreign into their academic studies" and " our research has our own characteristics". This is also the sum total of Mr. Chen's academic experience to integrate ancient and modern China and abroad, and to improve academic innovation. At the suggestion of Mr. Chen, Fudan University established an annual tradition of hosting the "Anniversary Symposium" which aims at promoting an excellent learning environment and the formation of university spirit from 1954.

▲ 50年代，陈望道与学生们在一起

▲ 陈望道发表在1955年校报上的《高等教育的奋斗目标》

▲ 陈望道与苏步青（左三）、谈家桢（左二）、蔡祖泉（左一）、刘洁（右一）开会照片

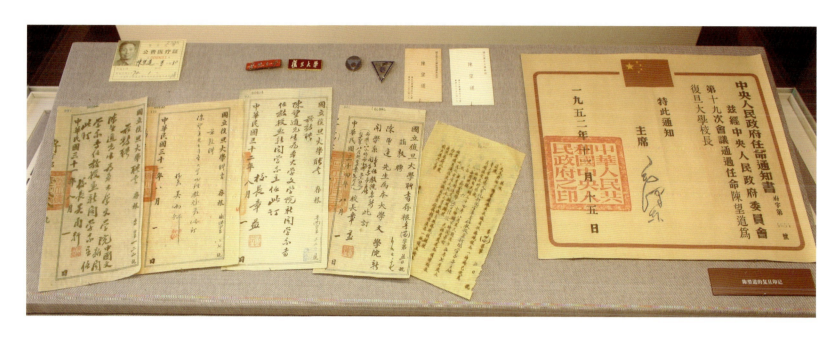

- 从左到右、从上到下依次是：陈望道的公费医疗证，陈望道题写的复旦大学校名徽，毛泽东题写的复旦大学校名徽，1949年前的复旦大学校名徽两枚，陈望道名片两张，毛泽东签发的任命陈望道为复旦大学校长的通知书，1949年前陈望道作为复旦大学中文系教授、新闻系主任的聘书存根。

千秋巨笔　一代宗师

- 从左到右、从上到下依次是：第一届全国人大代表当选证，第二届全国人大代表当选证，全国政协第一届全体会议代表证，全国政协第三届全国委员会第三次全体会议出席证，中国科学院学部成立大会出席证，华东军政委员会全体委员会议纪念手册，华东军政委员会文化教育委员会副主任任命通知，华东行政委员会委员任命通知；第三届全国人大代表当选证，上海市第二届各界人民代表会议代表证，全国文教群英会上海代表团出席证，中国作家协会会员证，中国科学院哲学社会科学部委员聘任书，华东行政委员会文化教育委员会工作证；中共十大签到证，上海市第二届各界人民代表会议第二次会议代表证，第四届全国人大代表当选证，上海市第三届各界人民代表会议代表证，国务院科学规划委员会语言学组副组长聘书。

全国综合大学会议合影（1953年9月22日）

第一次华东高等教育会议合影（1950年10月29日）

中华人民共和国第一届全国人民代表大会第一次会议合影（1954年9月21日）

千秋巨笔　一代宗师

精神财富　SPIRITUAL WEALTH

「风范」
DEMEANOR

● 生平厅之三（原为旧居藏书室）

风雨同舟 相濡以沫
United despite hardships

- 陈望道和蔡葵志同道合，经自由恋爱，于1930年冲破旧俗，在女方家乡举行新式文明婚礼，一时传为佳话。蔡葵曾留学美国，主编《微音》《女青年》等月刊，著有《独幕剧ABC》《新道德标准之建立》等，译有《艺术的起源》《世界文化史》《强者的力》《梁上君子》等，有广泛影响。新中国成立后，陈望道和蔡葵在复旦大学相互扶持，教书育人，比翼双飞。

- Chen Wangdao and Cai Kui cherished the same ideals, and after a period of courtship, they got married and held a modern wedding in the bride's hometown in 1930 regardless of old customs, which was widely viewed as a beautiful story at the time. Ms Cai had studied in the United States and acted as chief editor of monthly magazines such as *Wei Yin* and *Young Women*, is the author of *The One-Act ABC*, *The Establishment of New Moral Standards* and so on, and translated into Chinese *The Origin of Art*, *The History of World Culture*, *The Power of the Story Man* and *The Gentleman on the Beam*, etc., which have wide influence. After the foundation of People's Republic of China, Chen Wangdao and Cai Kui supported each other at Fudan University. As educators, they were regarded as an exemplar of a loving couple.

▲ 陈望道与夫人蔡葵

关怀后学 师生情长
Cherish one's juniors: a friendly teacher-student relationship

• 陈望道始终把学生放在第一位，爱生如子。"一师风潮"中，学生被军警包围在操场上，哭声震天。陈望道疾步走入学生中间，高声喊道："同学们，我和你们永远在一起，你们不要哭。"不少学生在他指引下走上革命道路。在白色恐怖下，他总是想方设法保护学生，1931年为此被迫离开复旦大学。对于青年学生的成长，陈望道一直极为关心，努力帮助他们解决生活困难，为他们指明人生方向。他和很多学生，如施存统、夏征农、倪海曙等，都保持着长期深厚的亦师亦友的情感联系。

▲ 陈望道与学生胡裕树（左一）、杜高印（左二）

• Mr. Chen always put the students in the first place, and he loved his students as if they were his own children. During the "Zhejiang No. 1 Teacher's College Incident", students were surrounded by military guards on the sports field and cried like thunder. Mr. Chen came forward and joined the crowd of students, and shouted loudly, "My students, I will always be with you. Don't cry". Under his guidance, many students chose the path of revolution. During the White Terror, he always tried his best to protect his students, and because of this, he was forced to leave Fudan University in 1931. Mr. Chen was always concerned about the growth of young students, and made efforts to solve their problems and show them the right path. He and many of his students such as Shi Cuntong, Xia Zhengnong and Ni Haishu kept a long-term relationship like friends despite the fact that he was their teacher.

诚心实意 砥砺同行
Sincerity and Honesty: move forward together

• 陈望道是"热水瓶"性格，待人诚恳，帮人做事无不尽力。他和鲁迅、刘大白、茅盾、郑振铎、夏丏尊、叶圣陶、丰子恺等诸多近现代文化名人都有很深的交往。上世纪五六十年代，一些老朋友在政治运动中受到冲击，陈望道总是热情劝导，鼓励他们努力工作，加强学习，不要丧失信心。对自己，陈望道则是高标准严要求，年事已高仍不放松党性修养，坚持"以老当益壮的精神为社会主义革命和社会主义建设努力""把心交给党，交给人民，交给社会主义"。

▲ 陈望道拄拐杖

• Although Mr. Chen looked cold outside, he was warm-hearted and always treated people with honesty and helped others as far as he could. He had profound relationships with many famous literary figures such as Lu Xun, Liu Dabai, Mao Dun, Zheng Zhenduo, Xia Mianzun, Ye Shengtao, and Feng Zikai. In the 1950s and 1960s when some of his old friends were implicated in political movements, Mr. Chen always comforted them and encouraged them to work hard, study hard, and never lose heart. Chen Wangdao was very strict with himself. Even in his later years, he never relaxed on his party principles, and persisted in "contributing to socialist revolution and socialist construction" and "dedicating his life to the Party, to the people, and to socialism".

千秋巨笔　一代宗师

书香留芳 BOOK COLLECTIONS

● 藏书室（原为旧居藏书室）

千秋巨笔 一代宗师

- 1958年，复旦图书馆（今邯郸校区理科图书馆）新楼建成，陈望道校长带领师生组成搬书人龙搬运图书进馆。他先后向学校捐书2400余册。1977年，学校图书馆制作了《陈望道校长赠书清册》，长达91页。

- In 1958, the new library was built. President Chen joined the teachers and students in moving the books. He donated more than 2,400 books to the university, the list of which covers as long as 91 pages.

▲ 1958年图书馆搬迁图

▲ 陈望道教授使用的樟木箱（该箱为1946年抗战胜利从渝返沪时使用，箱内展示书籍为《修辞学发凡》有关版本）

▲ 陈望道旧居樟木箱（箱内展示书籍为陈望道收藏的复旦五六十年代部分课件讲义）

▲ 陈望道旧居樟木箱（箱内展示书籍为北京红展馆赠予本馆200本各语种《共产党宣言》的精选版本）

珍藏手迹 MANUSCRIPTS

● 手札室（原为旧居卧室）
在陈望道诞辰一百周年的纪念活动中，领导人、著名学者和复旦同仁挥毫题辞，怀念他的精神。

陈望道手札（系1942年陈望道申请一级教授履历表的一部分）

久任教员奖金案内，道蒙列入十年以上一等之内，实则道自民八回国以后，即历任各大学教授，至今二十馀年，从未间断。计曾服务有：私立复旦大学（十一年半）、上海大学（四年）、持志大学（四年）、安徽大学（半年）、国立劳动大学（一年）、东吴大学（一年）、广西大学（二年）、国立复旦大学（二年馀）。其间有相重复者，除去重复，亦在二十年以上。惟抗战以来证件散失，是否可为晋等之请求？敬祈裁夺为幸。敬复

校长室

陈望道二月廿五日

 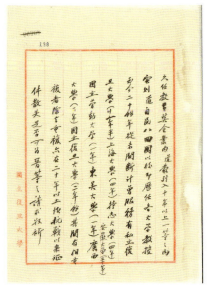 

玖园一隅　好学力行

CORNER OF THE 9th GARDEN, SPIRIT OF THE GREAT PRESIDENT

玖园一隅 好学力行

THE GREAT MASTER 大师望道

● 车库影院（原为旧居车库）

―― 玖园一隅 好学力行 ――

「影片《大师·陈望道》」

▲ 车库影院内播映：《大师·陈望道》（上海文广传媒集团纪实频道《大师》系列纪录片）

影片《信仰之源》

▲ 车库影院内播映：《信仰之源》（复旦大学新闻学院与上海文广传媒集团纪实频道合作摄制纪录片）

玖园一隅 好学力行

真理味道 TASTE OF TRUTH

◀ 铜像泥塑过程

▲《真理的味道》铜像（作者：唐世储）

玖园一隅 好学力行

▲ 油画：《真理的味道》（作者：俞晓夫）

玖园一隅 好学力行

字字珠玑 FAMOUS REMARKS

▲ 我是个偶像崇拜者，人类便是我的偶像。
——晓风（陈望道）（1921年）

▲ 大众语就是大众说得出、听得懂、看得明白、写得顺手的语言。
——陈望道（1934年）

▲ 好学力行
——陈望道为新闻系定立系铭（1943年）

▲ 优良学风的形成，是一个需要长时期的思想上启发和行动上实践的问题。
——陈望道（1963年）

▲ 活着一天就要为党工作一天。
——陈望道（1974年）

玖园一隅 好学力行

国福路51号
No. 51 Guofu Road

▲ 1958年校刊中刊载的旧居外观图

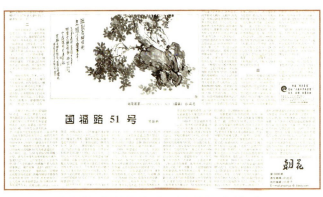
▲ 陈望道之子陈振新关于旧居的回忆文章

▲ 现旧居门牌

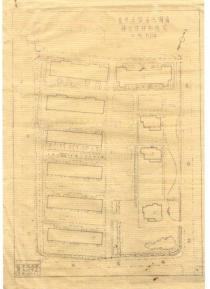

▲ 1977年，陈望道去世，其子女搬离旧居，旧居用作学校外国专家楼。2018年，为纪念马克思诞辰200周年、《共产党宣言》发表170周年，旧居改建为《共产党宣言》展示馆，作为复旦大学校史馆的专题馆，面向公众开放

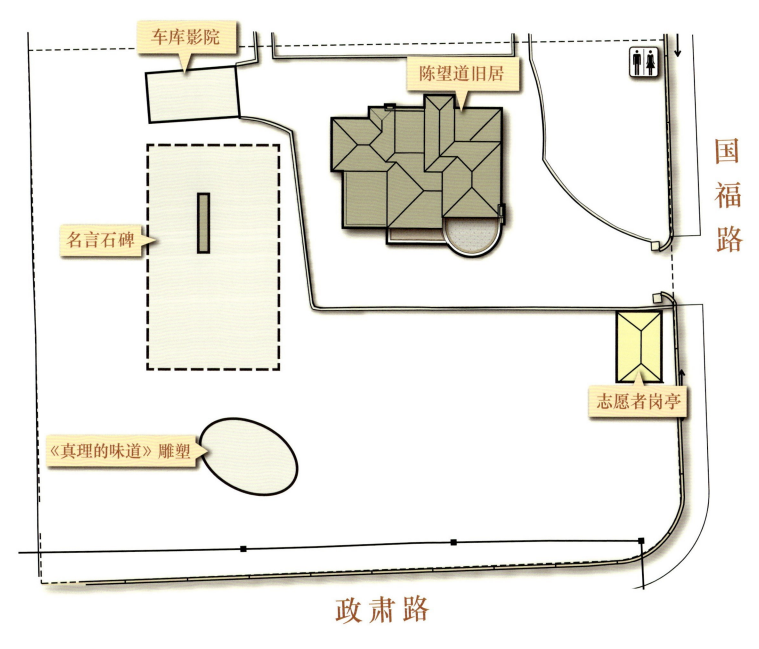

● 陈望道旧居室外平面图

● 陈望道旧居观众流线图

「结　语」

• 自《共产党宣言》问世以来，国际共产主义和社会主义运动波澜壮阔，马克思主义始终闪耀着不息的真理光芒。在中国共产党领导下，近代以来久经磨难的中华民族迎来了伟大复兴的光明前景，科学社会主义在中国焕发出强大的生机活力。《共产党宣言》作为一代又一代共产党人永恒的信仰之源，必将激励我们不忘初心，牢记使命，永远奋斗！

「EPILOGUE」

• Since *The Communist Manifesto* was published, the international communist and socialist movements have been growing immensely under the guidance of the eternal truth of Marxism. Under the leadership of the Communist Party of China, the long-suffering Chinese nation now sees the prospect of a great national revitalization, and scientific socialism has been full of vitality in China. As the source of unshakeable belief for the CPC of different generations, *The Communist Manifesto* will forever encourage us to remain true to our original aspiration, keep our mission firmly in mind and strive for the great success of socialism with Chinese characteristics in a new era!

图书在版编目(CIP)数据

宣言中译 信仰之源:汉、英/复旦大学档案馆编. —上海:复旦大学出版社, 2020.5 (2021.5 重印)
ISBN 978-7-309-14875-6

Ⅰ.①宣… Ⅱ.①复… Ⅲ.①《共产党宣言》-马恩著作研究-汉、英 ②陈望道(1890-1977)-传记-汉、英 Ⅳ.①A811.22 ②K825.46

中国版本图书馆 CIP 数据核字(2020)第 026925 号

宣言中译 信仰之源:汉、英
复旦大学档案馆 编
出 品 人/严　峰
责任编辑/李又顺
内文设计/尤　优

复旦大学出版社有限公司出版发行
上海市国权路 579 号　邮编:200433
网址:fupnet@fudanpress.com　http://www.fudanpress.com
门市零售:86-21-65102580　　团体订购:86-21-65104505
出版部电话:86-21-65642845
上海雅昌艺术印刷有限公司

开本 787×1092　1/12　印张 10.5　字数 157 千
2021 年 5 月第 1 版第 3 次印刷

ISBN 978-7-309-14875-6/A・45
定价:168.00 元

如有印装质量问题,请向复旦大学出版社有限公司出版部调换。
版权所有　侵权必究